TRUE PARENTING

Second Edition

TRUE PARENTING

Second Edition

Kathy Hayward

True Colors, Inc. Publishing
Santa Ana, California

True Colors, Inc. Publishing
3605 W. MacArthur Blvd. Suite 702
Santa Ana, CA 92704

Cover graphics by Michael Church
Typography by www.SunriseBooks.com
Editing by Larry Barkdull

ISBN: 1-893320-25-1
Library of Congress Control Number: 2001089732

To all parents
searching for tools
to make their families
stronger and happier.

ACKNOWLEDGMENTS

A popular definition of insanity is "doing the same things in the same ways but expecting different results." It is a saying worth every parent's consideration. Having the courage to learn new techniques has helped me fill my "tool box" with skills that enhance both my personal and parenting lives. There are many people whom I wish to thank for sharing their "tools" with me.

My special thanks to Don Lowry, whose ingenuity and energy have enlightened me and changed the way I look at the world. By introducing me to his innovative way of "colorizing" those whom I care about, Don has given me new ways to look at my relationships.

My thanks to Joe Sullivan and Fred Leafgren for sharing hours of advice that made me a confident True Colors® trainer. Thanks, also, to Bill Oliver for his down to earth advice in the area of parenting for prevention. Thanks to Cliff Gillies and Larry Barkdull for their expert guidance throughout the writing process, and to John Butler for his belief in my abilities to put this information in book form. Thanks to all the parents in my parenting classes and True Colors workshops who have, throughout the years, shared with me their challenges and their triumphs.

A special thanks to my husband, Ken, my daughters, Cherie, Shannon, and Susie, and to my stepsons, Connelly and Richard. They were always, and remain, my inspiration to improve my parenting skills. I continue to learn from them and for them.

About True Colors

"True Colors has been empowering individuals to succeed for over 20 years. True Colors works because it's simple, enjoyable, and based on true principles. Successful people seem to know who they are, what their True Colors are, what their values, needs, strengths, and joys are. They know and trust themselves, and behave accordingly. They appreciate the needs and strengths of others, and behave compassionately. Their integrity inspires trust—and productivity—in everyone around them.

"When you know what your core values and needs are, and feel good about them, you can perform at your highest potential in every area of life. And when you share a working, mutual understanding of others' core values and needs, you have the basis to communicate, motivate, and achieve common goals with utmost dignity, effectiveness, and mutual respect."

—Don Lowry,
creator of *True Colors*

Table of Contents

Chapter 1

In The Beginning

True parenting takes as much proficiency, understanding, and knowledge as any responsibility we take on in life. Yet the ability to parent is often assumed to be present from birth, and skills learned as needs arise. In this book we will examine our True Colors Spectrum and learn how it influences the way we raise our children.

Let's begin with a just a few fundamental understandings that make "parent decisions" successful.

Accepting the fact that children are not small adults is a critical beginning for any parent. A child is only on a journey toward adulthood; he hasn't arrived. Just like you and I, children gradually learn to copy adult behavior. Ever observant, the child is also learning to "parent"—good or bad. Here are a few realities:

- Your child has the need for self-confidence, a characteristic widely recognized as the basis for successful behavior.
- Your child will develop particular character traits as he assumes "roles" in his life. It is a parent's pride to observe that "my child's individual character is unique from others'."
- Even though basic characteristics are different, distinct similarities arise among groups of people. The adage, *birds of a feather flock together*, is accurate.

- Caring communication fulfills a child's needs for self-confidence, respect of self, worthiness, and self-esteem. Listening is a learned skill, not an inherited one.

True Colors has proven to be a vocabulary through which parents and children communicate their characters. It is an easy way to begin to understand ourselves and others. As we identify our true parenting character, we discover an invaluable tool for enjoying success in our personal life as well as in family and other relationships. Here are a few True Colors basics:

- Each of the four colors referred to in this book communicates a built-in idea. The color becomes a positive message.
- Colors are used to identify four distinct perspectives and personalities. Each color represents an individual's positive characteristics.
- All four True Colors constitute a character spectrum. Just as an actor "shades" a character role, we often call upon our least dominant colors to shade our relationships.
- The shading of colors adds dimension to our characteristics. Families build "rainbows" by appreciating the unique characteristics of each member.

In this book we will examine our color spectrum and learn how it influences the way we handle our children.

We, today, are experiencing the impact of the changing face of parenting. Good vs. Bad is far more nebulous today than in times past. Even the word "bad" in today's lingo can mean "good." How confusing can that be to young children? These days, bad guys win as often as good guys, and it's hard to tell them apart. Television has migrated from *Leave It to Beaver* to

South Park with moral issues being trivialized. Sex and violence on prime time television are portrayed as everyday occurrences, and few of us are shocked any more. In the old movies, good guys always wore white hats and won; bad guys always wore black hats and lost. Good vs. Bad was consistent.

Parents are primarily responsible for the way their children develop physically, emotionally, and spiritually. The ways in which parents nurture their children predicts what kind of people those children become. It all starts with the way you, the parent, instill values in your children. You are the main predictor of their success in school, how they choose a career, how they handle marriage, etc. That is a heavy load for today's parents.

The word "parent" used to be a noun, something that we are. In today's world the word "parent" has become a verb: something that we do. We have gone from having a passive title to a very active job.

In just two generations, parenting has changed. In the past, parents had the support of school, church, community, and the media. The same value messages were given by all. Society was encouraged to conform to social norms. Most parents knew what they were supposed to do. And because up to three generations often lived under the same roof, young parents had the guidance of the elders when they were not sure how to handle child rearing.

In the 1960's, great social reform occurred. Norms were tested and overturned. The "ME" generation lived the philosophy: "If it feels good, do it." Suddenly parents were told to allow children freedom of expression and that nonconformity was healthy. Sex, drugs, and Rock & Roll dominated society's attention. Rock & Roll became a culture—the guiding force for many young people, preaching sexual freedom ("just love one another") and drug use ("expand your mind"), were "with it" and the "now" things to do.

What are parents to do? "Modern" parents began allowing their children far more freedom than they had received as children. Moreover, society became far more mobile, and often the new generation of parents did not have the advantage of their own parents' living near to provide support.

Eventually the children of the 60's became parents. More confusion came with the reality: "It once felt good to me, but I can't do it any more, because I now have the responsibility of this child." Suddenly it wasn't just "ME" anymore. Serious questions emerged: "Do I now teach my children, 'If it feels good do it'? What if it doesn't "feel good" anymore?"

Not having grown up in a self-disciplined or value-driven generation, many new 60's parents found themselves struggling to teach their children discipline. True Colors offers some answers. Consider these questions:

- How can we raise our children to become self-sufficient?
- With society going in many different directions and social norms being nondescript, what do we teach our children?
- How do we keep our children safe from the craziness?
- Can we go back to the days when everything was predictable and we knew right from wrong?
- And who, back then, made the determination what was right and what was wrong?

Although the 1960s was, in many ways, a confusing time, some good came from those years. Issues like women's rights and racial equality come to mind. Parenting should be an equally important issue, but it often does not receive the deserved attention. In a nation of nonconformists, we should develop a measure of conformity, especially when it comes to the expectations we as parents have of our children. As a nation, we should be nurturing societal change to strengthen families. We can enjoy diversity without eliminating norms. Let us not, for example, accept children committing adult crimes. Let us not accept children having children. Let us not accept "entertainment" that is sexually provocative, particularly that which targets children as the audience.

As our nation wishes for a kinder environment, parents must assume the responsibility to determine family norms of behavior. Let us concentrate on strengthening the family. In this book we will focus on strengthening each member of the family by determining, honoring, and communicating each member's TRUE COLORS.

True Colors helps us recognize, for example, that the button-pushing child is probably a "primary Gold," one who functions best under consistent rules. The *never–sits-still* may be releasing his "active Orange" self for the moment. The *totally-off-the-wall* just might be seeking a "Blue's" need for recognition. The *thinks-so-much* is being a "natural Green" non-conformist.

As we will learn, real parenting success comes from our children's using their primary color strengths and brightening their second, third, and least-like-me character traits. Rainbows are made of such things.

As a parent, have you ever asked yourself these questions?

- What's going on here?
- Am I going crazy?
- Have aliens have taken up residence in our home?
- Is God playing some sort of joke on me?

- Has my mother's wish come true? You know the one: "When you grow up, I hope you have children JUST LIKE YOU!!" (Actually, that's probably the one thing that *didn't* happen and why we feel confused: they are *not* just like us!)

In my dealings with hundreds of parents during parenting education classes, I frequently hear serious concerns. My suggestions are: understanding your temperament and the temperaments of your children help bring perspective. Understanding temperaments can gives insight into why parents and children have trouble understanding each other. We each tend to see the world through our own "colored" glasses. Thus, we think, feel, and react.

Family therapy pioneer, Virginia Satir, said, "Once a human being has arrived on this earth, communication is the largest single factor determining what kinds of relationships he makes with others and what happens to him in the world around him."

Communication is vital to the happy, successful growth of the human spirit.

Chapter 2

THE THEORY BEHIND TRUE COLORS

The hypothesis behind ***True Colors***® is not new. (A theory of personality typing using four basic categories is historically summarized in the chart that follows.) It can be traced back twenty-four centuries to the Greek physician, Hippocrates, who identified four types of human beings: the Choleric (angry, cantankerous, peevish, irate, testy); the Melancholic (dejected, despondent, gloomy, morose); the Sanguine (buoyant, cheerful, hopeful, optimistic, sunny); and the Phlegmatic (languid, lethargic, listless, indifferent, passive).

After Hippocrates, the Greek philosopher Plato picked up on the same theme and described four basic types of people: the Artisans, the Guardians, the Philosophers, and the Scientists. A long list of scientists, philosophers, and psychologists throughout history echoed this same idea: people can be classified according to four clearly identifiable patterns of behavior.

In recent times the pivotal work came from the famed psychologist, Carl Jung, who described personality or temperament differences as "a fundamental basis for understanding human beings." His book, *Psychological Type,* culminated twenty years of research and included studies of ancient oriental astrologers, mythology, philosophy, literature and personal interaction. A psychiatrist, Jung studied reactions of his clients, and his research included many of their experiences. Jung came to believe that although people are different, they share common instincts, or temperaments, which influence how they function.

When Jung's work was translated into English in 1923, it had a profound effect on Katherine C. Briggs, who had been studying for years the differences in people. As a result, Briggs and her daughter, Isabel Briggs-Myers, developed the *Myers-Briggs Type Indicator (MBTI),* which is still used worldwide. Their theory refines the four personality types into sixteen sub-types. The MBTI is used frequently in corporations and other organizations in an effort to more efficiently use the workforce in a manner that is most comfortable and successful to the individual. Given the costs of training today, big business wants to ensure that its employees are suited to the job for which they are applying so that training dollars are not wasted. The MBTI is also used in counseling, to help clients understand human differences, and in education, to address specific learning styles and career choices.

During the past thirty-five years, David Keirsey has refined the work of Myers-Briggs. In his publication *Please Understand Me,* he condensed the Myers-Briggs sixteen types down to four temperament types, which are surprisingly similar to Hippocrates' and Plato's four types.

Don Lowry, a student of Keirsey, created the *True Colors* metaphor to translate these complicated personality theories into practical information we can all understand and use both in our personal lives and at work. He gave each of the four personality types a "color" and developed an easy-to-use set of tools that many and varied organizations have been using successfully since 1978. Lowry's primary purpose is to promote understanding among all people, which will foster improved relationships, diversity acceptance, and optimal personal performance, whether in the workplace, the home, the school, or the community.

The following table gives a brief overview of the history and evolution of personalty theories:

Examples of Personality Theories and Classifications

Hippocrates	Sanguine (Optimistic)	Melancholic (Pessimistic)	Choleric (Passionate)	Phlegmatic (Detached)
Plato	Artisan	Guardian	Philosopher	Scientist
Myers	Perceptive (SP)	Judicious (SJ)	Feelingful (NF)	Thoughtful (NT)
Keirsey	Dionysian (Artisans)	Epimethean (Guardians)	Appollonian (Idealists)	Promethean (Rationals)
Lowry	Orange	Gold	Blue	Green

On the next few pages, we will begin to define our own Color Spectrum. The first activity will give us insight into ourselves. This is your book; feel free to write in it. Or, if you wish, use a separate piece of paper to answer questions and make notations.

Chapter 3

Discovering Your True Colors

Now you are ready to begin discovering your True Colors. We will do several exercises to make this discovery. Your insights may change as we go through the process or you may recognize your True Colors immediately. Since our "colors" are part of what makes us unique, how and when we discover our spectrum is part of the being different.

It is important that we understand and accept our personal True Colors and those of our family members. Recognizing our colors increases our self-esteem and helps us accept those people with whom we share our life.

Relax, have fun, and follow the simple instructions for the exercise. Remember, all perceptions and answers are correct. If you find yourself having trouble choosing between answers, select the answer that is most correct for you most of the time. Take your time, feel free to review answers and change them at the conclusion of each exercise. The objective of True Colors is to "Know thyself," and that takes time.

At this point, please turn to the inserted personality cards that are bound into this book. Remove the cards from the book, and examine the four pictures. As you look carefully at the details, determine which picture you perceive "as most like me." Mark your first color below. Next, determine the one that is second "most like me." Mark it. Then, your third color. Your fourth becomes your "least like me."

Orange ______ Gold ______

Blue ______ Green ______

Now answer the following questions to gain insight into your colorful personality and to determine your Color Spectrum.

What Are Your True Colors?
Personal Questionnaire

Imagine yourself in the following situations, make note of (or circle) the letter of the response that is most like you.

If I won the lottery, the first thing I'd do with the money would be to:

A. Throw a big party
B. Put it in the bank for family and heirs
C. Share it with friends and relatives
D. Create a new venture or fulfill an ambition

2. When disaster strikes, I:

A. Laugh it off and move on
B. Am emotionally distraught
C. Make the best of it
D. Figure out why it struck

3. I tend to be more interested in:

A. Arts and crafts
B. Business and law
C. Literature and humanities
D. Science and engineering

4. My idea of a great vacation is:

A. A white-water rafting adventure

B. A traditional family vacation

C. A spiritual retreat or romantic getaway

D. A scientific expedition

5. I tend to seek relationships based on:

A. Excitement and adventure

B. Comfort and security

C. Romance and love

D. Shared intellectual interests

6. My ideal work space tends to be:

A. Free-form and fun

B. Organized and neat

C. Friendly and cozy

D. High-tech and efficient

7. What I value most is:

A. Action

B. Loyalty

C. Friendship

D. Intelligence

8. I tend to make decisions based on:

A. Impulses and whims

B. Past precedents and procedures

C. Feelings and emotions

D. Logic and research

9. If an extra-terrestrial appeared at my front door, I'd likely:

A. Grab and capture it

B. Close the door and call the cops

C. Try to befriend it and invite it in

D. Ask where it was from and how it got here

10. If I could be anything I wanted, I'd likely be:

A. An actor or artisan

B. A chief executive

C. A spiritual guru

D. An inventor

11. I tend to work best when I am:

A. The leader of the team

B. In a structured organization

C. With people I like

D. Left on my own

12. The words that best describe the *real me* are:

A. Bold and adventurous

B. Practical and dependable

C. Warm and compassionate

D. Competent and knowledgeable

Using the key on the next page, determine which color was represented most by your answers.

How many times was your answer (A) Orange? ________

How many times was your answer (B) Gold?___________

How many times was your answer (C) Blue?___________

How many times was your answer (D) Green?___________

My Color Spectrum

(write in the colors in order of dominance)

___________	__________	________	__________
(dominant color)	(second color)	(third color)	(lowest color)

Your answers determine your "color spectrum." The color you chose most frequently is your dominant color. As you consider your color spectrum from your most dominant to your least dominant color, you will begin to see a visual image of yourself emerging—those traits that temper your actions, your preferences, likes and dislikes. We are all made up of combinations of these four colors, and all four colors play important roles in our behavior.

A word about your fourth color. It often describes behaviors for which you may be criticized. You may experience misunderstanding and even conflict with someone whose first color is the same as your last color or whose last is your first.

The following describe the characteristics of each color.

Spontaneous Orange

I am spontaneous. I act on a moment's notice. I see life as a roll of the dice, a game of chance. I need stimulation, freedom, and excitement. I am a natural leader, troubleshooter, and performer.

I like to do things that require variety, results, and participation. I often enjoy using tools. I am competitive and bounce back quickly from defeat.

I value action, resourcefulness, and courage. I am generous, charming and impulsive. I show affection through physical contact.

At work, I am bored and restless with careers that are routine and structured, and satisfied in jobs that allow me independence and freedom while using my physical coordination and my love of tools. I view any kind of tool as an extension of self. I am a natural performer.

In love, I seek a relationship with shared activities and interests. With my mate, I like to explore new ways to energize the relationship. As a lover I need to be bold; I thrive on physical contact. I enjoy giving extravagant gifts that bring obvious pleasure to my loved one.

In childhood, I had the most difficult time fitting into academic routine. I learn by doing and experiencing rather than by listening and reading. I need physical involvement in the learning process and am motivated by my own natural competitive nature and sense of fun.

Orange–My Strength is my Skillfulness

I need freedom to take immediate action! A zest for life and a desire to test the limits best expresses my nature.

I take pride in being highly skilled in a variety of fields. I am a master negotiator. Adventure is my middle name.

I prefer a hands-on approach to problem solving, and a direct line of reasoning creates the excitement and the immediate results that I admire.

My keys to personal success are:

- The impulse to really live.
- Testing the limits.
- The need for variation.
- Excitement and light-heartedness.
- Charged adventure.
- Being a natural entertainer.
- Spontaneous relationships.
- Taking off for somewhere else.
- Being able to act in a crisis.
- A love of tools.
- Charm, wit, and fun.
- Being temporarily effected by defeat.
- Considering waiting as emotional death.

I see myself as adventurous.

I see life as one big party to enjoy. I live in the here and now, for who knows what tomorrow may bring?

I am always ready for a business deal or a deal of any sort, loving competition, and never missing an opportunity. My impulsiveness drives everything I do.

I am symbolized by the flight of the eagle, the sensation of riding a motorcycle, the roaring of the rapids, and the skillfulness of a virtuoso.

With Orange as my brightest color, I tend to:

- Dream of freedom, being spontaneous.
- Value skills, grace, finesse, and charisma.
- Regard opportunities, options, and competition.
- Dislike rigidness, authority, and use of force.
- Express optimism, impatience, eagerness, and confidence.
- Foster recreation and fun.
- Respect skills and artistic expression.
- Promote stimulation and risk.

The following items are the most mentioned by Oranges in *True Colors* workshops:

VALUES	NEEDS	JOYS	STRENGTHS
Adventure	Action	People	Independence
Excitement	Humor/Fun/Play	Fun/Humor	Flexibility
Spontaneity	Variety	Performing	Works well in crisis
Risk-taking	Freedom	Excitement	Gets things done
Flexibility	Challenge	Thrills	Resourceful
Uniqueness	Hands-on activities	Adventures	Energetic
Independence	Flexible environment	Creating	Open-minded
Success	Mobility	Winning	Sense of humor

Responsible Gold

I am responsible. I am the pillar of strength and have high respect for authority. I like to establish and maintain policies, procedures, and schedules. I have a strong sense of right and wrong. I am naturally parental and dutiful.

I do things that require organization, dependability, management, and detail. I need to be useful and to belong. I am the sensible, stable backbone of any group.

I value home, family, status, security, and tradition. I seek relationships that help me ensure a predictable life. I am caring, concerned, and loyal. I show concern through the practical things I do.

At work, I provide stability and can maintain organization. My ability to handle details and to work makes me the backbone of many organizations. I believe that work comes before play, even if I must work overtime to complete the job.

In love, I am serious and tend to have traditional, conservative views of both love and marriage. I want a mate who can work along with me, building a secure, predictable life together. I demonstrate love and affection through the practical things I do for my loved ones.

In childhood, I wanted to follow the rules and regulations of the school. I understood and respected authority and was comfortable with academic routine. I found it was the easiest of all the types of children to adapt to the educational system.

Gold–My Strength is Duty

With Gold as my dominant color, I value order and cherish the traditions of home and family. I provide for and support the structure of society.

Steadfastness and loyalty are my trademarks. Generous and parental by nature, I show I care by making everyone do the right thing.

To disregard responsibility of any kind never occurs to me.

My keys to personal success are:

- Generosity.
- Work ethic.
- A parental nature.
- Ceremony.
- A sense of history.
- Dignity, culture.
- Perpetuating heritage.
- Steadfastness.
- A value of order.
- Predictability.
- Home and family.
- Establishing and organizing institutions.

I esteem myself by behaving responsibly.

Be prepared is my motto. I enjoy the status and security that being prepared represents.

I have an instinct for keeping the product in production, for maintaining the structure, and for supporting the rules.

I have a strong awareness of right and wrong, with respect for the *shoulds* and the *should-nots*.

Symbols of strength—the flag, the preservation of honored institutions, the purity of home and family–describe me.

With Gold as my dominant color, I tend to:

- Dream of assets, wealth, influence, status, security.
- Value dependability, accountability, responsibility.
- Regard service, dedication.
- Dislike disobedience, non-conformity, insubordination.
- Express concern, stability, purpose.
- Foster institutions and traditions.
- Promote groups, ties, bonds, associations, and organizations.

The following items are the most mentioned by Golds in *True Colors* workshops:

VALUES	NEEDS	JOYS	STRENGTHS
Loyalty	Stability	Family	Organized
Perfection	Consistency	Home	Committed
Dependability	Order	Order/neatness	Consistent
Responsibility	Being on time	Status/security	Loyal
Honesty	Rules & Procedures	Volunteering	Practical
Order	Recognition	Hard Work	Law abiding
Consistency	Respect	Achievement	Reliable
Punctuality	Being productive	Job Satisfaction	Diligent

Compassionate Blue

I am compassionate. I am always encouraging and supporting. I am a peacemaker, sensitive to the needs of others. I am a natural romantic.

I like to do things that require caring, counseling, nurturing, and harmonizing. I have a strong desire to contribute and to help others lead more significant lives. I am poetic and often enjoy the arts.

I value integrity and unity in relationships. I am enthusiastic, idealistic, communicative, and sympathetic. I express my feelings easily.

At work, I have a strong desire to influence others so they may lead more significant lives. I often work in the arts, communications, education, and the "helping" professions. I am adept at motivating and interacting with others.

In love, I seek harmonious relationships. I am a true romantic and believe in perfect love that lasts forever. I bring drama, warmth, and empathy to all relationships. I enjoy the symbols of romance such as flowers, candlelight, and music, and cherish the small gestures of love.

In childhood, I was extremely imaginative and found it difficult to fit into the structure of school life. I reacted with great sensitivity to discord or rejection and sought recognition. I responded to encouragement rather than to competition.

Blue–My Strength is Authenticity.

With Blue as my dominant color, I seek to express the inner me. I value authenticity and honesty above all other characteristics.

I am sensitive to subtlety and, with flair, I create roles in life's drama. I enjoy close relationships with those I love and I possess strong spirituality in my nature.

Making a difference in the world is easy for me because I cultivate the potential in others and myself.

My keys to personal success are:

- Authenticity as a standard.
- Seeking reality.
- Devotion to relationships.
- Cultivating the potential of others.
- Assuming creative roles in life's drama.
- Writing and speaking with poetic flair.
- Self-searching.
- Having a life of significance.
- Sensitivity to subtlety.
- Spirituality.
- Making a difference in the world.
- Seeking harmony.

I see myself as being sincere and sympathetic.

With Blue as my dominant color, I am a person of peace and love. I am the natural romantic in life, idealizing the perfect moment and gestures of love.

I am most satisfied when nurturing the potential in others, bringing out the best in them. I am a facilitator of human potential.

The dove of peace, the romantic ballad, the drama of life, and the importance of a simple touch or handshake symbolize me.

With Blue as my dominant color, I tend to:

- Dream of love, affection, authenticity.
- Value compassion, sympathy, rapport.
- Regard meaning, significance, identity.
- Dislike hypocrisy, deception, insincerity.
- Express vivacity, enthusiasm, inspiration.
- Foster potential growth in people, harmony.
- Respect nurturing, empathy, sharing of feelings.
- Promote development in others.

The following items are the most mentioned by Blues in *True Colors* workshops:

VALUES	NEEDS	JOYS	STRENGTHS
Friendship	Understanding	Romance	Communicative
Compassion	Harmony	Hugs	Creative
Honesty	Hugs	Groups	Supportive
Sensitivity	Love	Music	Non-judgmental
Sharing	Affection	Affection	Optimistic
Love	People	Love	Intuitive
Caring	Inspiration	Nature	Accepting
Spirituality	Warmth	Friends	Understanding

Conceptual Green

I am conceptual. I have an investigative mind. I am intrigued by questions such as, "Which came first, the chicken or the egg?" I am an independent thinker, a natural nonconformist, and live life by my own standards.

I like to do things that require vision, problem solving, strategy, ingenuity, design, and change.

I value knowledge, intelligence, insight, and justice. I enjoy relationships with shared interests. I prefer to let my head rule my heart. I am in control of myself. I do not express my emotions easily.

At work, I am conceptual and an independent thinker. For me, work is play. I am drawn to constant challenge in my career, and like to develop models, explore ideas, or build systems to satisfy my need to deal with the innovative. Once I have perfected an idea, I prefer to move on, leaving the project to be maintained by others.

In love, I prefer to let my head rule my heart. I dislike repetition, so it is difficult for me to continuously express feelings. I believe that once feelings are stated, they should be obvious to a partner. I am uneasy when my emotions control me; I want to establish a relationship, leave it to maintain itself, and turn my energies back to my career.

In childhood, I appeared to be older than my years. I focused on my greatest interests, achieving in subjects that were mentally stimulating. I was impatient with drill and routine, questioned authority, and found it necessary to respect my teachers before I could learn from them.

Green–My Strength is Knowledge

With Green as my dominant color, I feel best about myself when I am solving problems and when my ideas are recognized, especially when I feel ingenious.

I seek to express myself through my ability to be an expert in everything.

My idea of a great day is to use my know-how like a laser to cut through and create solutions, since I am a complex individualist with great analytical ability.

Although I do not express my emotions openly, I do experience deep feelings.

My keys to personal success are:

- Developing models.
- Abstract thinking.
- Analytical process.
- Exploring ideas.
- Variety of interests.
- Striving for competency.
- Admiring intelligence.
- Storing wisdom and knowledge.
- Being a perfectionist.
- Abhorring redundancy.
- Using precise language.
- Handling complexity.

I esteem myself by using ingenuity.

With Green as my dominant color, I have a curious mind. To control the realities of life, I explore every facet of a problem or idea.

I am global-thinking by nature, always seeking universal truth.

I acquire skills and perfect any product or system on which I choose to focus.

Abstract thinking, the unknown challenge of outer space, the complexity and simplicity in design, and the symmetry of forms all describe me.

With Green as my dominant color, I tend to:

- Dream of truth, perfection, accuracy.
- Value answers, resolutions, intelligence, explanations.
- Regard efficiency, increased output, reduced waste.
- Dislike injustice, unfairness, superficial silliness.
- Express coolness, calm-and-collected reservation.
- Foster inventions and technology.
- Respect knowledge and capability.
- Promote effectiveness, competence, and know-how.

The following items are the most mentioned by Greens in *True Colors* workshops:

VALUES	NEEDS	JOYS	STRENGTHS
Intellectual achievement	Autonomy	High achievement	Creative thinker
Logic	Knowledge	Recognition of ideas	Strategist
Knowledge	Accuracy	Meeting a challenge	Problem solver
Facts	Data/Information	Solving a problem	Logical

(Continued from p.27)

VALUES	NEEDS	JOYS	STRENGTHS
Time to think	To find out how things work	Probing the future	Cool, calm, collected
Competency	Peace and quiet	Asking questions	Analyst
Creativity	To be understood	Creating strategies	Independent
Clarity	To question	Designing systems	Clear thinking
Quiet time	Space	Time to just think	Big picture

Chapter 4

DISCOVERING YOUR PARENTING STYLE

Now that you are familiar with the characteristics of the different personality types, we will turn our attention to parenting styles. Our parenting techniques come from many different sources. We learn some by imitating our own parents; we acquire some through parenting classes; we develop most through trial and error. Some techniques are consistent with our innate personalities, or "Colors." Still other techniques are acquired when we step outside the boundaries of our "Primary Color," sometimes making our parenting "color" different from our "Primary Color."

Using the True Colors models, consider the following to discover which parenting style is most like yours.

Orange

As an Orange parent, I am optimistic and flexible. I live in the present. I believe the purpose of life is to enjoy it. I do not spend a lot of time in long-term planning. I welcome and seek change. I can work in depth on things that I consider to be important. I enjoy sharing adventure and new experiences with my family. I like a home atmosphere that is relaxed and casual. I prefer a friendship style of parenting. I expect obedience from my children. I do not like dealing with family activities that require a lot of planning. I like to be free to pursue my own interests. Since I tend to be impulsive, I can be quick to anger when stressed, and just as quick to get over being angry.

Other family members do not easily manipulate me. I am realistic in accepting what exists without needing to be judgmental.

As Orange parents we...

- do not endorse a specific parenting style as the "right style" nor do we compare our parenting to others.
- separate well from the children when necessary.
- use humor when faced with deep topics.
- allow our children autonomy and like our children to be courageous and adventuresome.
- are comfortable in allowing others to participate in the raising of our children.
- enjoy being active and having fun with the family.
- believe in a practical hands-on approach to problem solving that produces immediate results.
- are willing to try new and creative things in order to solve a problem.
- use direct methods of communication in the family.
- do not make a fuss if family members are not extremely neat.
- expect our children to be the best they can be in whatever they pursue.

Gold

As a Gold parent, I am the caretaker of the family. I want to be viewed as responsible, hard-working, and dedicated to my family. It is important to me to do the right thing in my parenting role. I expect all members of the family to keep their word and respect deadlines. I believe in "work before play" and expect the family to follow this rule. I have opinions on how family members should behave and I can become upset when they do not act as expected. I like things to be done in a timely, organized and dependable fashion. I believe each member of the family should carry a fair share of responsibility. I prefer an authoritative style of parenting where children naturally respect and obey their parents. I desire my children to grow up to be responsible, hard-working, and to do right things.

As Gold parents we...

- feel responsible to see that family members "keep on task" and do the right things.
- need to feel appreciated for all we do for the family.
- feel it is our duty to establish rules and routines for the family to follow.
- see things as either right or wrong. We like facts and specific information.
- have strong security needs for the family.
- are family-oriented and expect others to uphold family traditions.
- want to be viewed as good parents.
- expect family members to be orderly in their environment and behavior.
- show that we love our family by doing things for them.
- will "do it ourselves" when others fail to meet an obligation or duty.
- when change must occur, we want it in an orderly and efficient manner so that things are stable and consistent.

Blue

As a Blue parent, I nurture the family's needs. Supporting the true potential of my children is fulfilling to me. I have a need for family cohesion through communication and emotional connections. I am a devoted parent and put a lot of energy into taking care of and trying to please my family. I am sensitive to perceived rejection from others. I value self-expression and thrive on being an important part of my children's development. It is important to me that my children develop positive self-esteem. I prefer to use a personalized and democratic style of discipline that involves other family members in a spirit of cooperation. I want my children to grow up and be happy with their lives and with who they are. I want each family member to feel they are unique and special to me.

As Blue parents we...

- desire a warm and affectionate home environment centered around people.
- are an enthusiastic and dramatic spokesperson for the family unit.
- are verbal and enjoy family members listening to us and to each other.
- enjoy the home as a cozy, comfortable and supportive setting.
- are emotionally sensitive to family situations and attempt to avoid conflict or competition.
- often take on the role of "friend-in-need-rescuer."
- can be inconsistent and subjective in handling our children, depending upon how we feel at the time.
- often put other family members' needs before our own.
- are sometimes torn between feelings about what needs to be done and what we feel good about doing.

Green

As a Green parent, I encourage intellectual potential. I want my children to grow and develop with motivation emanating from within themselves. I want my children to develop to their fullest creative potential and be competent at whatever they choose to do. I encourage my children to investigate and ask questions about subjects that interest them. I enjoy having intellectual discussions with family members. I like to explain the reasons behind making important decisions and try to influence other family members to make informed decisions. I view quarreling with my children as a waste of time that drains everyone's energy. I often use a "lecture" atmosphere to help my children understand the importance of thinking about their actions and the consequences. I prefer a logical and objective style of parenting in which children are rewarded for their achievements.

As Green parents we...

- expect other family members to at least attempt to achieve the same intellectual standards they set for themselves.
- want our children to have the desire to obtain knowledge without external manipulation.
- believe acquiring knowledge and improving one's mind should be a primary goal for all family members.
- focus our energies on future learning and improvement.
- desire to communicate with family members in a clear, concise, and informative manner.
- may not praise easily and may appear unemotional, using critique as a constructive tool in order to improve a situation.
- dislike wasting time on the mundane.

- naturally seek answers to life's questions and expect our children to do the same.
- view learning as its own reward.
- believe natural curiosity will lead our children into the right career.
- expect all family members to respond logically to any given situation.

A Quick Parenting Colors Discovery Check

Used as a starter to determine your True Color parenting style, here is an easy self-check. All answers are correct; one fits your style best. Honesty will be the most accurate "colorizer" of your personal style and parenting spectrum. In each set of the four categories, determine whether A, B, C, or D is most like you. Read all four sentences. Circle the letter, or record it on a separate sheet of paper.

Set 1

A. I think children should fit into my schedule, not me into theirs.

B. I feel an awesome responsibility to teach my children all the little but important things in life in order that they will always look their best and make the right decisions.

C. My children are very special to me and I don't look forward to their leaving home.

D. I think children should be self-motivated, and I try to stay out of their way.

Set 2

A. Children should participate in all the activities they can, as long as they're good at them.

B. I spend a lot of time keeping the home clean and neat, and children should have their responsibilities, too.
C. I want my children to enjoy their home, be comfortable here, and invite all their friends to visit.
D. If children have questions, they can come to me for the answers until they learn how to find the answers themselves.

Set 3
A. I want my children to be noticed.
B. I expect my children to behave.
C. I want my children to be happy.
D. I expect my children to remain in control of their emotions; their tears put me off.

Set 4
A. I want to have fun with my children and actively participate in their lives.
B. Children should know the rules and follow them to the letter without question.
C. I like it when my children are emotional and come to me for support. I like to help them.
D. My relationship with my children is most comfortable when we are on an intellectual level.

Set 5
A. "Live each day as if it were your last" is my motto.
B. "Be prepared" is my motto.
C. "To thine own self be true" is my motto.
D. "Think about it" is my motto.

After each letter/color, list the total number of times you selected it from the five sets. By referring back to the definitions of each color, this self-discovery chart will give you a basic idea of your dominant preferences and parenting style.

A. Orange________ B. Gold________ C. Blue________ D. Green________

Chapter 5

YOUR "OTHER HALF"

By now you see that you and your spouse (or companion) likely have different temperaments and therefore approach life and parenting uniquely. It is important to recognize a co-parent's differences. Often we choose companions who are different from us, who can easily do those things that we struggle with. Although we admire them for their abilities, they may also make us "crazy" because of our differences. For example, an Orange husband may appreciate that his Gold wife always pays the bills on time, runs an organized home, and can always find his keys. But he may become frustrated when she wants him to hang up his clothes as soon as he takes them off, or insists that he wash out the garbage cans every week, or that she becomes angry when he leaves the cap off the toothpaste.

Different parenting styles not only cause problems between parents but also total confusion for children. When the parents are not presenting a united front, the children have a hard time deciding what the rules are. Factor in the child's own unique temperament, and home can become a battlefield. The good news is that with the "language" of True Colors, even parents with divergent color spectrums can work together to determine how best to rear their child, according to the *child's* color. The challenge, of course, is to educate both parents so that they can develop a plan for parenting that is acceptable and comfortable for them both.

Comparisons between family members' personal color spectrums can provide insight into the sources of family conflict. Personality Color spectrum and Parenting Color spectrum may or may not be the same. Although our personalities are innate, our parenting skills are learned through imitation, education, and trial and error. You should consider your combined Personality and Parenting color spectrums in order to visualize consistencies and inconsistencies in yourself and your partner. For example, I happen to be a person whose color spectrums are different. My Personality spectrum is Orange/Blue/Gold/Green, but my Parenting spectrum is Gold/Blue/Orange/Green. This means I react differently to my friends than I do to my children. Toward my children, I am more conservative in my expectations. I feel more concern that my children follow the rules that I set for them than I do that my friends follow society's rules. My home life is much more structured than my social life. Refer to the exercises and information above to fill out the following chart for you and your spouse or companion.

Your Personality Color Spectrum

____________	____________	____________	____________
Dominant Color	**Secondary**	**Third**	**Lowest**

Your Parenting Color Spectrum

____________	____________	____________	____________
Dominant Color	**Secondary**	**Third**	**Lowest**

Co-parent's Personality Color Spectrum

__________	__________	__________	__________
Dominant Color	**Secondary**	**Third**	**Lowest**

Co-parent's Parenting Color Spectrum

__________	__________	__________	__________
Dominant Color	**Secondary**	**Third**	**Lowest**

Color Spectrums

As you consider these color spectrum combinations, it is valuable to understand that they describe how a person acts and reacts. For example, a Gold/Blue parent will see things differently than a Gold/Green parent, even though their dominant color is the same. It is through these combinations that we find both our commonalities and our differences, and are more able to compromise.

My husband and I, for instance, are very different in our color spectrums. I am Orange/Blue/Gold/Green and he is Green/Gold/Blue/Orange. Notice that my dominant or first color is his last and his first color is my last. So how do we manage to have a very happy, stable, and compassionate relationship? My Orange and his Green sides both have strong needs for freedom and independence; my Blue and his Gold sides hold to the firm belief that our family is the core of our existence. So, although we each "go our own way" in many aspects of our lives, we know and trust that our marriage and family are the most important. We "connect" through the commonalities in our colors rather than "diffuse" because of the differences. We trust each other to enjoy the freedom we need, knowing that we have no reason for jealousy or fear in our relationship. We also recognize each other's strengths and use them to the best advantage for the family. When one of our children needs help with math or science, they go to Green/Gold Dad; when they need help in literature or social studies, they come to Orange/Blue Mom. For guidance in finances and long-range planning, they go to Green/Gold Dad; for guidance in relationships or encouragement to take a risk, they come to Orange/Blue Mom.

Children pick up on this concept far more easily than do adults. In many cases they have not yet learned to be skeptical or untrusting. They go by instinct.

Chapter 6

PARENTING YOUR CHILD IN THE "RIGHT" COLOR

A key to better parenting is to learn to parent your child in ways that naturally compliment your child's core temperament. This means having an understanding of his unique needs, his values and beliefs (based on the four temperament colors), and being able to communicate these things to your child.

In some cases, a child's "colors" are easy to identify. Others' are not so evident since children, like adults, are combinations of all four colors. As you begin to identify your child's colors, watch for opportunities to help him experience the needs, values and beliefs of all the colors in order to develop an understanding and tolerance of others. The next few pages will be valuable in understanding the behaviors that indicate a child's primary color. The studies of patterns, tendencies of behavior, and temperaments associated with each "color" have been adapted from David Keirsey's book, *Please Understand Me*, as applied in the True Colors publication, *Resource and Reference Guide.*

Orange Children

Orange children are apt to be active babies. Their desire to perform is their highest priority. Their need for attention will dominate the day. They will prefer to roam rather than be confined in a playpen. They likely enjoy animals but may tend to be too rough with them. They are also rather hard on both toys and clothes and should be given sturdy, well-made objects. Simple games and objects are likely to hold their attention more than complicated ones.

Orange children are likely to be very active. They generally enjoy food and are called "good eaters," though they don't like to be confined too long in a highchair or at the table. They also tend to get into messes rather quickly. Leave them in the yard even for a moment and they somehow manage to get dirty. This leads to a scolding; however, they learn early to be indifferent to such scoldings, for these come too frequently.

Orange children are less likely than others to understand demands for clean rooms or orderly closets. Their rooms are likely to be a jumble of toys, clothes, and valued objects, all in disarray. But to these children, everything is just as they want it. They are "too busy" to want to take time to hang up and fold clothes. And, "Anyway," they would say, "What difference does it make?" They see these things as a waste of time when they could be off doing something that is FUN!

Orange children can be excellent team players. They thrive on competition. Equality and liberty are very important to them. They like to talk with others but have a need to control their own activities. Unless they have full control over whatever project they undertake, they are likely to lose interest as others "interfere." To engage Orange children, you must entertain them. They do not learn well when asked to sit still and listen. They must be active in using or making something. Whenever possible it is good to get them excited and let them take risks.

Orange children should be recognized for their performance. They are likely to feel good about themselves and about their parents if they are provided a great deal of room to move and be active. At home, lectures and reading activities should be short. They do not enjoy activities that must be done quietly and alone. They want chances for action in an area of personal interest. Drama and performing are exciting and help meet the need for action.

While Orange children need to practice concentration—dealing with complex things or delaying gratification—they will develop this ability best when their natural preferences for action, avoidance of complexity, and tolerance for delay are recognized first, or given as rewards for completing a task.

Orange children believe that today is to be lived for the excitement it brings; tomorrow can be left to take care of itself. Therefore they find little sense in statements that urge them to have distant goals, to study hard in order to prepare for work or further education, to save pennies to guarantee the future, to make plans in order to get ahead, or to develop social ties to have a place in society.

Gold Children

Gold children respond happily to a well-established, clearly defined routine. They, more than other children, need to know that what is so today will be so tomorrow. Constant changes, confusion, and crises cause them pain. Frequent residential changes can be unsettling. They feel most secure when raised with friends who grew up with them in the same neighborhood, school system, and community.

Gold children are more vulnerable to family instability than others. To be caught between one parent who is strict and one who is lenient can be devastating. They seek the security of parental firmness, agreement, and consistency. They want things to rely on so they can trust certainty.

Gold children thrive on relating to their extended family—aunts, uncles, grandparents, cousins, and so on. They like to visit with relatives and get tremendous enjoyment from the traditional holidays such as Christmas and Thanksgiving. They enjoy stories of family history and remember these histories when they grow up. Gold children do well in a large family, and having brothers and sisters usually is a source of gratification to them.

Gold children enjoy having routines and respond to the assignment of specific responsibilities such as emptying the wastebaskets, taking out the trash, sweeping away the grass or snow, tending a small garden, or cleaning their room. They need tasks within their ability to perform and perform well, but enjoy routine maintenance chores at home and at school. They value orderly closets and their bureau drawers are apt to contain neatly folded clothes. Toys are arranged in order on the shelves.

Gold children get pleasure from adult approval as they perform the tasks assigned. This constant feedback is vital to them. The task, as an end in itself, soon loses appeal if adult approval is not forthcoming. Being right or wrong is important to them. They want to do things in the "right way," that is, the way which will please the adult in charge. They also respond to scolding and negative criticism, under which they tend to try all the more. They pay attention to details and hold high standards of achievement for themselves and for others.

Gold children learn better when shown a new skill in step-by-step order, being asked to demonstrate small segments. They need to know what is expected of them, and they need to be certain how to accomplish the task. They enjoy checklists. They thrive on routine. Crafts appeal to them. They like to make things from wood, cloth, and yarn. The steps necessary to doing the project, however, must be done correctly. Work needs to be planned, scheduled, and carefully done. A gift of handwork from a Gold child should be appreciated and prominently displayed.

Gold children generally have a comfortable time growing up. They get along well if at least one parent is Gold, Green, or Blue, but might have some difficulty adjusting if they happen to have two parents who are Orange and are unpredictable.

Blue Children

Blue children, even at an early age, display a gift for language. They talk early, and seem to never stop talking. They may daydream a lot, and make up stories with imagery. They may be accused of lying when they are really only exercising their imagination.

Blue children seek a sense of self and see the world from a personal focus with themselves at the center. They often identify with characters in stories. They may be over-stimulated by stories of dragons, witches, etc. They usually enjoy being read stories that are beyond their own reading abilities but which spark their imaginative powers. They may want the same stories read over and over.

Blue children enjoy "people" toys—dolls or animals to which they can attach a personality. These toys become a real part of their life with stories and fantasies woven about them. A lost toy friend is a real tragedy, and ridiculing an imaginary friend by others may crush these children, for they may feel rejected themselves.

Blue children have a charm which draws people to them. They have a talent for relating socially with both peers and adults. They are apt to be hypersensitive to another's feelings.

Even if they are the winner, they feel badly for the loser. Rather than wanting to be competitive with others, these children prefer to be cooperative in game playing and competitive against themselves.

Sometimes Blue children are painfully shy and hypersensitive to even the slightest gesture or word of rejection. They tend to idolize others but will hate them with equal fervor if rejected or ridiculed. They thrive on an abundance of personalized attention and do not respond to physical punishment. They are hypersensitive emotionally to conflict. Interactions with peers have a great impact on Blue children. They may lack defenses against behaviors that others would handle easily, and they have difficulty handling the anger in themselves or in others. Their quest for self may cause them to find themselves out of step with other children.

Promises are important to Blue children. If commitments are not honored, they feel that neglect very deeply and take it personally. If this happens, they may, too often, develop physical symptoms, such as eating problems.

Blue children seek recognition each and every day and need to know that they are valued by those around them. Conflict at home is a source of discomfort. If they are reared in a home where the parents quarrel, they are apt to become withdrawn and insecure. In order to develop their own identity, they need the assurance that those around them are in harmony. The addition of a new family member needs to be carefully handled with Blue children, who are always seeking a sense of self and value as they look for their meaning in the world. They flourish in an atmosphere of love and harmony. Personal touch or physical closeness usually transmits love and warmth.

Green Children

Green children as infants may be rather solemn and are likely a puzzle to those around them who are not also Green. They may talk early and learn to read long before they go to school. Parents should provide them with a variety of toys that are appropriate for the child's age and social maturity, but only a few at any one time. They are likely to be deeply involved with a new toy for hours, contemplating how it is made, and then abandoning it and seldom again showing interest. They usually enjoy books and being read to longer than other children.

Green children are usually not interested in family rituals and traditions since they need reasons for doing things. They may need help in seeing that these are important events for other members of the family. They may be organized one time and messy the next, such as in the way they keep up their room and clothes. But they know where each and every treasure is placed. They tend to have extensive collections.

Green children often experience rejection from their peers at an early age. They frequently report their childhood experiences, saying, "I thought I was the only person in the whole world who was like me." They like to be given directions only once and become impatient with repetition.

Green children are apt to pepper a parent with *why* questions: "Why can't I fly like a bird?" "Why can't I have dessert before my vegetables if I eat both?" They pursue their curiosity-lust, wondering, "What would happen if . . ?", then proceed to try to find the answer, whether adults approve or not. "What would happen if I put my finger in the electric socket?" "What would happen if I put my bread in the water pitcher?" These children need abundant opportunities to experiment, discover, and find answers. None of these exploring behaviors is designed to annoy adults: their purpose is to satisfy the child's need to find out. Shutting off this experimental behavior is likely to result in disobedience and disruptive behaviors.

Green children generally are not the least bit interested in coming into conflict with those about them. If this happens as a result of their investigations, they are apt to accept the consequences impersonally. However, these children quickly lose respect for those who are not logical in their reprimands or who issue edicts that are not plainly justified by the circumstances. Physical punishment is deeply violating to these children, for they see this abuse as a violation of their nature.

Dignity is usually important to Green children. They are devastated by ridicule and sarcasm concerning their ability, for they want others to see them as competent. They are naturally self-doubting and need success. Due to their early interest in technology they may be asked about that which is beyond them. When they experience failure they are likely to retreat into themselves. They seldom respond well to negative criticism. However, they can be impatient and rude in rejecting the ideas and opinions of others, especially those they view as being beneath them intellectually. Parents should help Green children understand the impact of this attitude.

Chapter 7

Your Family Rainbow

List the colors of your personality Color Spectrum:

________	________	________	________
Dominant Color	**Secondary**	**Third**	**Lowest**

List the colors of your co-parent's personality Color Spectrum:

________	________	________	________
Dominant Color	**Secondary**	**Third**	**Lowest**

#1 Child's Personality Color Spectrum:

________	________	________	________
Dominant Color	**Secondary**	**Third**	**Lowest**

#2 Child's Personality Color Spectrum:

________	________	________	________
Dominant Color	**Secondary**	**Third**	**Lowest**

#3 Child's Personality Color Spectrum:

___________	___________	___________	___________
Dominant Color	**Secondary**	**Third**	**Lowest**

#4 Child's Personality Color Spectrum:

___________	___________	___________	___________
Dominant Color	**Secondary**	**Third**	**Lowest**

(You may have more than four children, or there may be other family members you would like to include. Record their colors here.)

Personality Color Spectrum for (name of person)

___________	___________	___________	___________
Dominant Color	**Secondary**	**Third**	**Lowest**

Personality Color Spectrum for (name of person)

___________	___________	___________	___________
Dominant Color	**Secondary**	**Third**	**Lowest**

Personality Color Spectrum for (name of person)

___________	___________	___________	___________
Dominant Color	**Secondary**	**Third**	**Lowest**

Personality Color Spectrum for (name of person)

____________	____________	____________	____________
Dominant Color	**Secondary**	**Third**	**Lowest**

Personality Color Spectrum for (name of person)

____________	____________	____________	____________
Dominant Color	**Secondary**	**Third**	**Lowest**

Take a good look at the overall color picture of your family. Do you have a rainbow? Are some colors dominant throughout? Are you the only one with your dominant color? Do you have a child whose colors are opposite yours? Are you and your companion similar in temperament? Can you spot some potential challenges?

Remember that your own parents influenced the way you perceive parenting, so it may be helpful to add their colors, too. Hopefully, you have gained insight into other relationships in your life: your siblings, co-workers, neighbors, and friends.

It is a truism that knowing something about what makes a person "tick" can help you understand and accept that person's behavior. It doesn't mean either of you are right or wrong, you are just different.

By using the TRUE COLORS system, your world becomes a more pleasant place to live. Value those who are different from you; appreciate their ability to do the things you cannot. Recognize people for their strengths instead of criticizing them for their "differentness." For example, identify the colors of those people closest to you and plan a party. Let each person take a part.

Need a theme? Ask a Green. Need decorations? Ask a Blue. Need to make sure you have enough of everything? Ask a Gold (They won't forget the toothpicks and garbage bags.) Need entertainment? Ask an Orange. When you all pull together and have a part, the party is bound to be a success!

A great project for the whole family could be planning next year's vacation. Start now with a family meeting to get suggestions. The feedback won't be the same from everyone. Ask everyone to think about it for a week, and then come back together for more brainstorming and prioritizing. Be sure you include everyone. Here is how you might expect it to play out:

Talking and thinking about vacation gives Oranges something to look forward to and helps pass the tedious days until vacation time comes. They may want to mark off the days on a calendar. This exercise can do a lot to teach them about delayed gratification. "Good things come to those who wait."

The Golds in the family will love preparing the itinerary and figuring out the costs. They will love developing job charts so that everyone can be earning money toward the vacation. They might even like scouting the neighborhood to find odd jobs for everyone (walking dogs for Orange, cleaning out the garage for Gold, babysitting for Blue, tutoring for Green).

Blues will begin to choose their wardrobe, gather cards to mail to friends, select a special memento to take along to remind them of home, decide what souvenirs to bring back to friends, and call everyone they know to tell them about the vacation. Blues may plan some special surprise to give to family members once the vacation has begun, or they may create small gifts for people they meet.

Once the family has decided where they will be vacationing, Green children will research opportunities and check out possible activities. They will enjoy determining which activities will best fit into the budget and still be enjoyable for the family. Allowing Golds to keep the records, you could develop a budgetary system with a time line to make sure the family is on track for saving the money they will need and staying within the budget. The family's Greens will love the system once they learn it. They will love to figure out who would enjoy what activities, and they will plan something for everyone. What a learning experience for your children!

Worried that there will be chaos? Count on it. Here are a few insights and tips that may help you all get along better, remembering that when you recognize and appreciate the primary colors of your co-parent and children, chaos can be turned to comfort.

Chapter 8

BUILDING FAMILY ESTEEM

Based on Don Lowry's booklet, *Building Family Esteem with True Colors*, let's examine some examples of how you might relate to your co-parent and children of the same or different dominant colors. Please note that for categorizing purposes, some information is duplicated.

So you are Orange. . .

"Knock, knock."
"Who's there?"
"Orange."
"Orange Who?"
"Orange you glad you got this book?"

If you are Orange, you are always ready with a joke or funny story. You are energetic and competitive, quick-witted, and impulsive. You are a natural entertainer and performer, and you desire variety. You are a problem solver and a master negotiator. You think quickly on your feet. You have a high need for mobility. As a parent, you are in control and don't take nonsense from anyone. You often handle discipline with humor, but the consistency depends on how your day has gone.

Two Orange co-parents definitely make a fun couple! You share the same values and interests. You both have energy to see things through. Neither of you take life too seriously. You may change your address frequently with job changes, and develop new friendships and interests. You may find that a challenge is your need for attention and that you are competitive enough to get it. Your secondary colors will come to play when someone has to pay the bills (you know, actually sit down and write out checks!).

Orange and Gold co-parents can make for a potentially volatile situation. You both like control but may have different value systems. The children may become confused and/or learn to play one parent against the other: "Mom said/Dad said." You must always be sure to discuss challenging issues with each other so you can present a united front, especially when it comes to discipline. The Orange parent will tend to be far more lenient with the children's undesirable behaviors than will with the Gold co-parent. Compromises will be necessary for family structure to be consistent. The Gold parent may choose to defer to the Orange parent the extra-curricular activities and take over the day-to-day events. The Orange parent is usually amenable to relinquishing responsibility.

If you are Orange and your co-parent is Blue, your Blue partner will do everything in their power to maintain a harmonious household. Blues are cooperative rather than competitive and are sensitive to the needs of others. Blue will defer to your stronger Orange personality, however, as long as the outcome is positive. Your Blue co-parent will receive great joy in watching you play with your children and will support you in most of your requests. Regardless of your color, you can rest assured that if your co-parent is Blue, your children will be nurtured and cared for. If you and your co-parent are a mix of Orange and Blue, the challenge may be in disciplining your children. Orange sees little need for discipline unless the offense is grave; Blue doesn't want anyone to be angry and often takes on the responsibility for the child's offense. ("The child broke the vase because *I* didn't put it away. It's really *my* fault.") But, all in all, Orange and Blue is a compatible couple and will have a fun-loving home.

If you are Orange and your co-parent is Green, you share a need for independence and will instill that need in your children. The Green parent takes a more hands-off approach, and will almost always defer to you the day-to-day parenting responsibilities. The Green parent may, however, become critical of your devil-may-care tendencies. Greens believe that life is serious and frivolity is to be frowned upon. Greens prefer to relate to the children on an intellectual level. Green parents will enjoy helping them with homework and school projects, for example. A Green co-parent will expect more from the children and have less interaction than you (Orange) do.

Orange parent and Orange child–this is a great match! You and your child share the same values, interests, and energy. Being of the same color group, you are compatible and easily understand each other. Parents and children of the Orange group tend to be very active, adventurous, and seek excitement. Both will compete and like hands-on activities. You are physical and spontaneous. Beware of competing against each other or creating situations of "one-upping" the other. The challenge for you, as an Orange parent, is to remain the "parent,"and not just become the "friend." Children need their parents to be parents. They need guidance from adults to feel secure in their environment. They need limits to ensure their safety. Enjoy, but remember your position as parent.

The combination of Orange parent and Gold child can be the biggest frustration to an Orange parent. Oranges have few rules and provide little structure for Gold children, who seek tradition, plans, and predictability. Gold children have a strong sense of right and wrong, and the parent's Orange lifestyle can appear "standardless." The playful attitude and spontaneous nature of the Orange parent is sometimes fun for Gold children, yet can be embarrassing to them. Both child and parent share a need for usefulness of ideas and objects. The cluttered home that the Orange parent provides may be unsightly to the Gold child, but not bother the Orange parent. Gold children tend to worry about the impulsive actions of the Orange parent. An Orange parent tends to worry about the fastidiousness of the Gold child and may habitually urge him to "Just have fun!" An Orange parent has to consciously remind himself that the Gold child *is* having fun–in his own way.

If you are an Orange parent and your child is Blue, your child will understand your need for adventure and your impulsive actions. The Blue child enjoys the Orange parent's fun-loving sense of humor but may get feelings easily hurt by the parent's to-the-point directness. The Blue child shares with the Orange parent the quest for possibilities, yet the Orange parent is the greater risk taker. The Blue child is not competitive and seeks cohesion, harmony, and cooperation. The Blue child may feel neglected by an action-oriented Orange parent. Because the Blue child is a "pleaser," the Orange parent may not notice the subtle nuances of his deep feelings. Nor may the Orange parent always understand the child's easy tears and emotional displays. An Orange parent may develop a way of minimizing a Blue child's dramatic responses to perceived rejection. A Blue child can learn a lot from the Orange parent's modeling of assertive behavior.

An interesting combination is Orange parent and Green child. Both value freedom and like to explore a variety of interests. The Green child thrives on ideas and invention, while the Orange parent seeks for adventure on a physical level. The Orange parent may laugh about the Green child's being too stuffy or being a bookworm; the Green child may laugh about the Orange parent's being too wild or "off-the-wall." A Green child and an Orange parent will reward each other with mutual respect, even though the Orange parent may not measure up to the Green child's drive for perfection. Because Orange is a natural performer, an Orange parent may call upon the child to "perform" for family and friends. The Green child may be willing to discuss an intellectual challenge or pet project, but is uncomfortable being the center of attention unless it is recognition for intellectual achievements.

Bold Gold–Tradition!

Gold is traditional, consistent, upstanding, loyal, scheduled, confident, and bold. If you, your co-parent, or your child is Gold, you are up to any task. Golds value order and status quo. Golds are conservative and stable, helpful and trustworthy. Golds believe there is a right way to do everything. Golds strive for security and a stable environment. If you are Gold, your parenting style is strict, with little room for flexibility. You probably chose to use a clean piece of paper to make notes about this book rather than to write in it.

If you are Gold and your co-parent is Orange, you have a potentially volatile parenting situation. You both like control but have different value systems. The children may become confused and/or learn to play one of you against the other: "He said/she said." You must always be sure you discuss challenges together so that you can present a united front, especially when it comes to discipline. You, Gold, will be far more affected by your child's undesirable behavior than your Orange co-parent. You will need to compromise for family structure to remain consistent. You may choose to defer to your Orange co-parent's desires for extra-curricular activities, while you take over the day-to-day responsibilities. Remember, Orange is usually very willing to relinquish responsibility.

If you are Gold and your co-parent is Blue, your companion will do everything possible to maintain a harmonious household. Blues are cooperative rather than competitive. They are sensitive to the needs of others. Your Blue co-parent will defer to your stronger Gold personality as long as the outcome is positive. Blue will receive great joy from your successes and will happily meet your requests. You (Gold) will enjoy knowing that your children are being nurtured, leaving you more free time. As a couple, you may find disciplining challenging–Gold insists on strict rules and logical, consistent, fair consequences, while Blue doesn't want anyone to be angry and often takes responsibility for the child's offense. ("He broke the vase because I didn't put it away. It's really my fault.") Gold may become stressed when Blue does not follow through on disciplining or consequences.

Two Gold co-parents: a Gold co-parent wants to manage the home so that everyone knows their responsibilities and expectations are realized. Gold will have a place for everything and everything will be in its place. Gold will see that schedules are confirmed, calendars coordinated, lists posted. Because Gold loves tradition, he/she will create family memories for their children to carry on. In a Gold parent's home there may be power struggles from time to time, but strong family values will allow Golds to share control fairly.

If you are Gold and have a Green co-parent and don't try to make him/her a neat freak, things will be fine. As a Gold, you will be able to find things! Something to remember: your Green co-parent hates social confrontation and will usually defer on the discipline of the children. However, a Green co-parent may debate decisions about discipline for hours, but it will be done in private. Green needs a private place to think and some alone time to process the day's events. Green likes change and modernization while Gold, on the other hand, craves stability and tradition. Green will relate to the children on an intellectual level, enjoying helping with homework and school projects. Green and Gold parents expect a lot from their children.

Another interesting combination is Gold parent and Orange child. There are often clashes with this mix. They have different value systems, for example. The Orange child is a risk taker who needs action, spontaneity, and adventure. The Gold parent holds to traditional values, morals, and a definite sense of right and wrong. The Gold parent treasures stability, responsibility, and predictability, and will have difficulty with the Orange child's impulsive fun-loving nature and need for immediate gratification. Orange children may rebel against his Gold's parents rules and his planned, serious approach to life. Therefore, the Orange child needs some input in the family rules, if he is expected to respect them. It will be a challenge for the Gold parent to allow the Orange child the freedom he feels he needs in order to thrive and become the best he can be. Compromises can come in the form of sports activities that are acceptable to both parent and child, whereby the Gold parent can feel assured that his Orange child is taking risks in a controlled environment.

Gold parent/Gold child: this is a Golden match! This combination satisfies and supports both the parent and child. Both enjoy the clearly defined expectations and rules of the house. Things are neat, orderly, and run on a schedule. The consistency and stability of the home is a comfort to both. Gold child and Gold parent mutually support and adhere to tradition and the laws of home and society. There is a clear sense of the parent being in charge. Much hard work occurs at home and both parent and child excel in work and school.

Another combination: Gold parent/Blue child. The Blue child will comply with the Gold parent's rules and structure at home. A Blue child may behave differently with friends, however, in order to be accepted. Both Gold parent and Blue child share the need to belong and are dependent on the family. The Blue child strives for harmony, while the parent expects adherence to right and wrong according to family rules. The Blue child's idealism and the Gold parent's realism sometimes clash.

Gold parents and Green children often clash. A Gold parent will want to instill in his/her children the values of planning for a secure future—savings, a dependable job, etc. The Green child will tend to value the quest for abstract, future-oriented ideas, anything that has to do with invention and mental challenge. Both a Gold parent and a Green child tend to approach life seriously and not take physical risks. The Green child is independent while the Gold parent wants to draw him into the family unit—more than the child desires. The Green child may rebel against the controlling nature of the Gold parent, since Greens have a need for *self-control*. A Green child's independent nature can be disruptive to the Gold parent's need for schedules. Green children have a need for change, whereas the Gold parent tends to become stressed by sudden changes.

True Blue Feelings

For either a Blue parent or a Blue child, tears can have many meanings. Blues cry when they are sad, when they are scared, when they are melancholy, when they are happy, when they are surprised. Blues cry over babies, animals, and the elderly. They cry over the injustices in the world, the abuse of animals and children. Blues cry at weddings, funerals, graduations, school plays, movies, and TV commercials. Blues want to save the whales, the trees, the endangered species, the oceans, and the children. If you are a Blue parent you are pretty lenient when it comes to discipline, and you have the hardest time letting your children grow up and become independent. You wish you could have them with you forever.

If you are Blue and your co-parent is Orange, you can expect that he/she will make you laugh and cry. (Often at the same time.) As a Blue, you will enjoy the antics of your Orange partner, who tends to take life with a grain of salt. You will admire his/her confidence and ability to make things happen. Blues are not competitive, so you will allow your Orange companion to be the center of attention in the home.

If, on the other hand, you are Blue and your co-parent is Gold, your home may take on this appearance: Your Gold companion will be comfortable with strict rules and sensible, consistent consequences. Your being Blue, however, means that you want no one to be sad or angry, especially the children. As seen by Gold, you may not fit into his/her image of a parent because you are nurturer while Gold is a disciplinarian. Your

Gold partner may become frustrated when you fail to follow through on consequences that he/she has administered.

Two Blue co-parents will have a home full of expressed emotion. You will both thrive on hugs and will like to touch and be touched. You both will also be physically loving with your children. Because neither of you will confront the other, you sometimes will let small incidents simmer until one of you explodes over something unrelated. You will need ongoing reassurance that you are loved, respected, and accepted by the whole family. Discipline may be sporadic and inconsistent, depending wholly on your moods, not on your children's behavior. If you and your co-parent are Blues, it would be helpful to write down some expectations for you and your children so that home management is more consistent.

If you are Blue and your co-parent is Green, remember: for Blues, everything has to feel good; for Greens everything has to make sense. This combination presents some interesting challenges. While Blue likes to express feelings, Green is very uncomfortable with emotions. Blue's tears will really put off Green, and Green will probably have to be alone after them to sort things out. In the meantime, you (Blue) may feel rejected, while your companion's (Green) only intention was to think things through and give you (Blue) time to get yourself under control. Blue/Green combinations need to consciously work on communication in order to maintain their relationship. A strong secondary color can help temper the sensitive Blue.

The Blue parent/Orange child combination is interesting. An Orange child may rebel against his Blue parent's need to communicate and relate. A Blue parent's push for honesty may be construed as intrusive to the Orange child's need for independence. The Orange child may view the Blue parent as a pushover. A Blue parent will encourage the Orange child's need for creativity, and may allow too much flexibility and not enough discipline for the Orange child. The challenge for the Blue parent is to remain in charge, realizing that providing structure will feel stressful, but is necessary for development of children. The Blue parent needs to remember that his/her child will someday be out in the world and will have to learn responsibility. It is better that the parent be the teacher than a stranger. If you are a Blue parent, set up some simple rules and consequences that are acceptable to you and that you know you can keep. Write them down so that you can refer to them when dealing with your children, particularly your *acting-out* Orange child.

Another combination is Blue parent/Gold child. If your child is Gold and you are a Blue parent, you share the values of belonging and helping others. Areas of potential difficulty involve the Blue parent's idealistic, searching, imagination, which conflicts with the Gold child's need for practical, outlined structure. Remember, the Gold child may see the parent as "wishy-washy" and as not providing enough "back bone" for the family. Often, the Blue parent's searching for uniqueness involves non-traditional activities viewed as curious to the Gold child. The Gold child may rebel outwardly, but will be suffering inside because of a strong sense of right and wrong. For example, a Gold child will feel that it is wrong to question the parent, but will be unclear as to the parent's expectations. This can create a great sense of discomfort for the Gold child. Again, writing out some rules and consequences can help both of you establish some consistency.

If you are a Blue parent and your child is also Blue, you will likely enjoy a satisfying relationship. Your compatible values meet your natural needs for communication, sensitivity, and understanding. Both of you will nurture each other's spiritual searching and creative expression.

If you are a Blue parent and have a Green Child, your child may feel smothered by your Blue need for communication, family cohesion, and emotional connections. These are uncomfortable for a Green and often seen as silly. A Blue parent's focus on fostering dependency on the family is the exactly opposite of the Green's quest for knowledge and independence.

It's Not Easy Being Green

If you are Green, you are a standard setter and a visionary. You are an idea person, philosophical and complex. You are competent and serious, a perfectionist. You can never know enough. You explore all facets before making a decision. You are in control of yourself. You are a loner, an intellectual, often not in the mainstream. You believe relationships, once developed, should maintain themselves. This all impacts on a Green parent's co-parent and their children. A Green parent believes that children need to be independent and it may be difficult for a Green to connect emotionally with his/her children.

A Green parent has a need for independence and will try to instill that trait in his/her children. If your co-parent is Green, and you are not, he/she will take a more hands-off approach to child rearing, and will almost always defer to you day-to-day parenting responsibilities. Your Green co-parent may, however, become critical if you have "devil-may-care" tendencies. Green believes that life is serious and frivolity should be frowned upon. Green prefers to relate to the children on an intellectual level and enjoys helping with homework and school projects. Your Green co-parent will expect more from the children than you will (if you are a different color) but will have less interaction with them. Then again, if you and your partner are Green, you are a compatible couple because you share the same values and needs. You respect each other's need for independence and space. You both strive for perfection. You stimulate each other's logic, inventiveness and wisdom. Your home may be a bit unconventional, but you should be comfortable there. Your challenge may be in who has control. You may not share well and may have to consciously divide the issues to be controlled.

Green parent's relationship with the other co-parent "colors" have been discussed previously in this chapter.

A Green parent and an Orange child share similar values of getting to the point. They are also similar in the drive to compete and feel competent. Difficulties arise when the Green parent's future-oriented, abstract thinking conflicts with the Orange child's drive for here and now action. The Green parent's controlling nature will probably be met with rebellion from an Orange child. Green parents try to instill a sense of internal motivation in the Orange child who, by nature, has an external locus of control.

If you are a Green parent and have a Gold child, he/she may have difficulty understanding your Green abstract thinking. The Gold child will want and ask for more detailed, organized, practical guidance. A Green parent's high expectations for perfection will motivate the Gold child to do well, yet may be perceived as too demanding after a reasonable standard has been met. This may leave the Gold child feeling it is impossible to measure up to the Green parent's expectations.

Green parent and Blue child is a combination that often leaves the Blue child starved for attention due to the Green parent's preoccupation with ideas, abstractions, and the need for independence. The Green parent's need to be distant from frequent emotional connections or demonstrations may leave the Blue child lacking in affection and interaction with the Green parent. The Blue child will strive to meet the Green parent's expectations in order to please, but the child may feel the Green parent is too demanding and that he/she is never quite good enough.

If you are a Green parent and have a Green child, you are a compatible combination, because you share the same values. You both stimulate each other's logic, inventiveness, and wisdom. You both strive for perfection, and feed off of each other's projects. There is a mutual respect for each other's need for independence. You are both powerful people, and you may experience clashes over each other's ideas. Your Green child may feel the need to be as good as or better than you, the Green parent; and you, the Green parent, may feel the need to maintain control.

Chapter 9

Improving Relationships

Considering the previous information, we can begin to apply the principles to relationships. Study the following suggestions to improve your *couple* relationship.

If you have an Orange partner:

- Recognize the need for freedom.
- Value playfulness.
- Help your partner to think before they act.
- Spontaneously play with them.
- Realize stress comes from lack of excitement.
- Reinforce optimism.
- Praise your partners skills.
- Respond to generosity.

If you have a Gold partner:

- Care about the need for security.
- Do some reasonable planning.
- Praise responsible actions.
- Remember sentimental moments.
- Acknowledge stability.
- Respond to important dates.
- Be on time.
- Respect the need for neatness.

If you have a Blue partner:

- Make romantic gestures.
- Have intimate talk.
- Recognize the need to contribute.
- Provide the warm touch and embrace.
- Reassure your loving commitment.
- Express your feelings.
- Be open and responsive.

If you have a Green partner:

- Recognize the need for independence.
- Value your partners abstract thinking.
- Preserve the privacy to think and to read.
- Accept the lack of romantic gestures.
- Realize stress comes from fear of looking foolish.
- Allow your partner to be self-critical.
- Understand that Greens esteem themselves by being competent.
- Praise with ingenuity.
- Help with day-to-day details.

Implementing these ideas will help you keep alive the love that brought you together in the first place. It will help you be a better couple and better parents. Don't let that original romance be lost. Have fun together. Laugh, cry, and enjoy each other as individuals. Take at least one week of vacation each year without the children. Try once a month to have a night out without parental responsibilities. Don't get stuck in your parenting roles at the expense of losing your relationship with each other. Spend time together as a couple.

Improving Sibling Relationships

Power struggles between siblings are often the result of what True Colors calls "Core color need conflicts." Compare, below, the core personality color spectrum of each child with that of siblings. Notice similarities and differences in the two first colors of the children in the family. Remember that power struggles between siblings are often the result of "core color need conflicts." Core color similarities between siblings usually enhance their relationship, while core color differences add additional stressors to the relationship and result in misunderstanding individual differences. Too often children compare themselves to one another without any knowledge of the influences that innate temperament differences play in their behavior at home and at school.

Age differences and birth order are also factors in sibling relationships, but we will focus here on personalities. It is important to teach your children to identify and understand the core color temperament for themselves and for each of their siblings. It is also important for your children to value each of the four temperament colors and realize that each child has been born with an innate "gift," which is something to be valued. A healthy family environment recognizes and encourages the children's True Colors to come shining through. Sometimes the family environment tries to force children to meet parental expectations and needs while denying the core needs of the children's innate identity. Families play a primary role in the development of an individual's self-image. Families influence nearly all aspects of an individual's existence, including personal relationships, attitudes toward different cultures, educational and career choices. Familial childhood interactions with members of an individual's family teach values, reinforcing which behaviors bring rewards and which bring consequences.

Parents set the mood for the family. This mood may have a strong influence on a child's behavior. When parents do not understand a child, the cause may be a core color conflict and therefore represent conflict of values, motivators, and esteem needs. Likewise, when a child is understood, the color codes may be alike or blended in a complementary way, resulting in common values.

Let's look at probable family reactions when different sibling color combinations are present. Understanding the motivations of your children's behaviors is the first step in learning how to meet their needs and reduce sibling rivalry and stress. (Please note that for categorizing purposes, some information is duplicated.)

The Orange Child's Relationships with Siblings

Orange child with Orange sibling: Two Orange siblings will spark each other's sense of adventure and playfulness. This combination is commonly found. They will often get into mischief together, as well as compete against each other, which appears to be a love-hate relationship. They often share the same values, interests, and aspirations. They are active (often viewed as hyperactive), spontaneous, and jokesters. They question or disregard rules and are out for fun.

Orange child with Gold sibling: This is a classic "core color conflict." The Gold sibling values rules, order, systems, planning, and predictability. The Orange child values freedom, few rules, risk taking, and adventure–exactly opposite those values of his Gold sibling. These children tend to clash on issues of responsibility: Gold sees Orange as irresponsible, while Orange views Gold as too serious, a "stick in the mud." The two seldom do things together or get along well. The Gold child tends to judge his or her Orange sibling negatively, and Orange tends to disregard Gold.

Orange child with Blue sibling: This combination works when the Blue sibling pleases the Orange. Yet, Orange's confrontational approach often hurts the feelings of the sensitive Blue child. Both share values of being with people and being imaginative. The Blue child, more than his Orange sibling, is both dependent and demanding in relationships. Orange strives for independence.

Orange child with Green sibling: With understanding, respect and parental support, this sibling combination can bond well. The Green sibling is interested in ideas and is independent in his or her work, while the Orange child is independent in an active, physical sense. Both are daring in their interests and respect each other's need for freedom. The Orange child sometimes chastises his Green sibling for not being more daring or energetic, while the Green can chastise his Orange sibling for acting before thinking.

The Gold Child's Relationships with Siblings

Gold child with Orange sibling: As stated above, this is a classic "core color conflict." The Gold sibling values rules, order, systems, planning, and predictability. The Orange child values freedom, little structure or rules, risk-taking, and adventure—exactly opposite his Gold sibling's preferences. These children tend to clash on issues of responsibility, the Gold sibling viewing the Orange as irresponsible and the Orange child viewing the Gold as too serious. These two seldom do things together or get along well. The Gold tends to judge the Orange in a negative way and the Orange tends to disregard the Gold.

Gold child with Gold sibling: This sibling pair works well together. They hold and perpetuate the same traditional values of family, society, right and wrong. If they believe in a different set of rules, they will experience conflict, with both being headstrong in their opinions. Gold/Gold siblings will not tend to get into much trouble, since they value rules, but they will tattle on those who break rules. They are loyal to each other and dependable.

Gold child with Blue sibling: This combination tends to get along well. Both have the need to belong and the need for security. The Gold tends to need security in the necessities of life, whereas the Blue's focus is on relationships. The Blue child strives to please others, thus the Gold sibling in the relationship may be the one in control. The Blue child may also get his feelings hurt by judgments made by the Gold child.

Gold child with Green sibling: These two tend to be fairly reserved in energy and risk-taking. They clash in the areas of being organized, efficient, and independent. The Gold sibling desires order, a clear sense of right and wrong, and working for future life security. The Green child thrives on innovative, abstract ideas and regards the future in terms of knowledge but not necessarily practicality. The Gold child wants to belong and upholds traditional values, whereas the Green sibling is independent and non-traditional in thinking.

The Blue Child's Relationships with Siblings

Blue child with Orange sibling: This combination works when the Blue sibling tries to please the Orange, yet the Orange's confronting approach often hurts the feelings of the sensitive Blue child. Both share values of being with people and being imaginative. The Blue child is more dependent and demanding in relationships than the Orange, who strives for independence.

Blue child with Gold sibling: This combination tends to get along well. Both have needs to belong and to be secure. The Gold tends to need security in having the necessities of life, whereas the Blue's focus is security in relationships. The Blue child strives to please others; thus, the Gold sibling may be the one in control. The Blue child may also get his/her feelings hurt by the judgmental Gold child.

Blue child with Blue sibling: This sibling combination works well. Both share the same values of relationships, pleasing others, communication, and creativity. They sometimes get so caught up in socializing that it creates problems in school or facilitates dependent relationships. Sometimes they feed off of each other's worries and can become so preoccupied with other people's opinions that they smother relationships. These two siblings are often inseparable.

Blue child with Green sibling: This combination tends to be strained. The Blue sibling's need for closeness and communication conflicts with the Green sibling's need for independence and distance from emotional connections. Often, the Green child will distance himself from the Blue, saying the Blue child is too illogical, emotional, or unstable.

The Green Child's Relationships with Siblings

Green child with Orange sibling: This sibling combination can work well. The Green sibling is interested in ideas and is independent in his/her work, while the Orange child is independent. Both are daring in their interests and respect each other's need for freedom. The Orange child sometimes chastises the Green for not being more daring or energetic, and the Green chastises the Orange for acting before thinking.

Green child with Gold sibling: These two tend to be fairly reserved in energy and risk-taking. They clash in values of being organized and independent. The Gold sibling desires order, a clear sense of right and wrong, and working for future life security. In terms of knowledge, the Green child thrives on innovative, abstract ideas about the future, although that knowledge may not necessarily be practical. The Gold child wants to belong and upholds traditional values, whereas the Green child is independent and non-traditional in thinking.

Green child with Blue sibling: As mentioned above, this can be a strained combination. Blue wants closeness, which conflicts with Green's wanting independence and distance from emotional connections. The Green child will distance himself from the Blue, saying the Blue child is too illogical, emotional, or unstable.

Green child with Green sibling: This is a workable combination. These two share the same values regarding ideas and the quest for intelligence and challenge. They are independent and may not do much together, yet will respect each other. They may compete, and conflicts may arise because of their drive for perfection and control. They will often debate each other.

Chapter 10

DEVELOPING PARENTING SKILLS

Now that we have examined possible familial color combinations, let's turn our attention to the development of skills that will help us in parenting.

Effective parenting skills to use with Orange children

Good communication with Orange children is:

- functional and operational.
- knowing just what words to use (the "in" words).
- impactful (strong, attention-grabbing).
- succinct—to the point.
- clever.
- changeable from topic to topic, but consistent in theory.
- punctuated with action, jokes, stories.

The self-esteem of Orange children is supported by:

- opportunities for self-expression.
- an audience.
- the chance to be active.
- opportunities to act quickly.
- novel experiences, frequent change.
- external excitement.
- the chance to show initiative and cleverness.
- opportunities to challenge the imagination.
- the development of a wide variety of skills.
- opportunities for leadership

- permission to make workable decisions without coming into conflict with the family's overall goals.
- freedom to defy risk, succeeding or failing without judgment or interference (unless danger is imminent).

Increase the motivation of Orange children by:

- focusing on immediate needs and issues.
- making tasks short-term, fun, challenging.
- allowing them to be expedient.
- giving immediate feedback/recognition on positive actions.
- providing hands-on activities.
- including experiential approaches to learning, such as with music, art projects, and dramatizations.
- providing games and a competitive atmosphere.
- providing opportunities for them to present themselves and their work to others (to show off).
- stating clearly the benefits of completing tasks.

Intervene and discipline Orange children by:

- offering incentives and hands-on rewards for positive behavior.
- setting ground rules, stating clearly the consequences for undesirable behavior, and sticking to those rules.
- using cool-headedness and a sense of humor to avoid anger.
- teaching the importance of moderation when they use their "Orangeness" as an excuse to defy authority; defusing defensive attitude by saying, "*Yes, but a wise Orange knows when to stop!*"
- acknowledging their needs, expressing appreciation and understanding for their preferences, while bringing them

back to reality by saying, with a sense of humor, "*I know you would rather be on your skateboard right now instead of being stuck cleaning your room, but let's see how we can make the best of this situation.*"
- reprimanding in private, but as immediately as possible. Explain clearly and with humor what they have done wrong.
- giving them "time out" periods when they become overly stressed.

Effective parenting skills to use with Gold children

Good communication with Gold children is:

- clear.
- precise.
- direct (matter-of-fact).
- to the point.
- decisive.

The self-esteem of Gold children is supported by:

- consistency.
- clear rules.
- opportunities to display responsibility.
- opportunities to be of service to others.
- concrete evidence of success (formal recognition, certificates, grades, etc.).
- opportunities for leadership.
- opportunities to organize things or people.
- being acknowledged as an important part of the family.
- clear and specific feedback *("I like the neat way you set the table.").*

Increase the motivation of Gold children by:

- providing the opportunity for them to assist in planning.
- addressing what has been done and assessing what needs to be completed.
- providing the opportunity for them to display leadership ability.
- giving them authority to organize others.
- asking them to set up schedules for goal attainment.
- offering suggestions that lead to increased productivity.
- maintaining stability, policy rules, consistency, and predictability.
- providing an atmosphere for "meaningful" chores.
- clarifying expected outcomes.
- providing consistent feedback.
- making rewards, an allowance, and special opportunities specific.

Intervene and discipline Gold children by:

- regularly acknowledging and praising good work and behavior.
- generating simple, clear, and fair family rules and expectations.
- posting rules and expectations in a conspicuous location.
- being clear about who is responsible for what and about when things are to be done.
- appealing to their strong sense of right and wrong.
- being consistent and making the punishment fit the crime.
- being fair and providing warnings and reminders.
- talking privately to find out what might be the root cause of the behavior.

- criticizing fairly in ways that do not diminish their feelings of self-worth. For example, you could say, *"Your room looks pretty neat, but I noticed several things left under the bed. They will have to be put away properly in order for your job to be complete."*
- reminding them, after the reprimand is over, how much you value them.

Effective Parenting Skills to Use with Blue Children

Good communication with Blue children is:

- personalized.
- honest.
- congruent with non-verbal communication.
- subjective.
- metaphorical.
- an opportunity to express and accept feelings.
- often warm and humorous.
- an opportunity to express acceptance, appreciation, and affection.

The self-esteem of Blue children is supported by:

- harmonious environment.
- acceptance and appreciation for who they are.
- personal recognition for accomplishments.
- opportunities to demonstrate their creativity.
- opportunities to communicate with and to encourage and support others.
- opportunities to please those in authority.
- opportunities to motivate others in the family.

Increase the motivation of Blue children by:

- allowing them to participate in making family plans.
- keeping them involved.
- offering numerous opportunities to work with other members of the family.
- keeping activities meaningful.
- emphasizing relationships between ideas and people.
- frequently telling them how good you feel about their achievements.
- giving them a hug or patting them warmly on the back.

Intervene and discipline Blue children by:

- clearly outlining your expectations in a friendly and frank way.
- acknowledging their need to interact with their friends.
- letting them know you care and are willing to listen.
- attending more to positive than negative behavior.
- asking for their opinions regarding what works best in changing undesirable behavior.
- talking to them one on one, then stopping for a few minutes to let your words "sink in."
- always hugging them after a reprimand to let them know you love them as a person, explaining that your remarks were only directed to their behavior.

Effective Parenting Skills to Use with Green Children

Good communication with Green children is:

- characterized by high-level vocabulary, analogies, and metaphors.
- logical and concise.
- focused on possibilities.

- non-redundant.
- devoid of small talk.

The self-esteem of Green children is supported by:

- positive feedback on the quality of their work, when deserved.
- abundant success.
- numerous opportunities to display competence.
- requests for contributions of their own findings and conclusions.
- expectations/duties that reasonably challenge them.
- providing answers for their innumerable questions.
- opportunities to increase knowledge and build competence.
- providing freedom to create some of their own responsibilities within the family.

Increase the motivation of Green children by:

- posing problems that they can solve independently.
- providing opportunities to display competency.
- encouraging them to create and evaluate.
- providing opportunities to assist in planning.
- requesting from them insight into the topic being discussed.
- acknowledging their good ideas and competent performances with sincere appreciation.
- giving only deserved positive feedback, avoiding fake hoopla.

Intervene and discipline Green children by:

- providing the logic behind the rules and recognizing their reluctance to blindly obey rules.
- allowing them to participate in formulating rules.
- understanding that when power struggles occur they are challenging your ideas more than they are challenging you.
- keeping your cool and stating clearly why a specific behavior is undesirable.
- reprimanding the behavior, not the person, and doing so only in private.
- avoiding the use of sarcasm and labels.
- discussing why it would be to their personal benefit to act differently.
- asking them to explain how their undesirable behavior could be modified.
- frequently recognizing what they are doing right socially rather than nit-picking at their less successful efforts.

Chapter 11

ADDRESSING THE NEEDS

Addressing the Needs of Orange Children

Orange children need an outlet for their energy. Often organized sports can be very helpful; sports offer physical activity while teaching children to follow rules, to become team players, and to accept consequences for breaking rules.

Living within the rules of society is often difficult for fun-loving Oranges. They often push those rules to the limit, just to see how far they can go and what they can get away with. For parents, it is very important to be consistent with discipline and also to recognize your Orange children's attempts at self-discipline. Use such statements as, "That must have been hard for you to complete your homework before turning on the TV. I know how much you enjoy your programs. I am proud of you." Recognizing their struggles may help them to overcome the desire to push every limit. They should not be allowed to use their "Orangeness" as an excuse for undesirable behavior.

Enjoy and praise your Orange children's ability to laugh and joke. Encourage their need to "perform" and recognize their courage in channeling the risks involved. Direct those risk-taking tendencies to activities that are safe and supervised.

Recognize your Orange children's strong will as an asset that will help them become unique individuals, leaders, not followers. Encourage their leadership tendencies with positive recognition and support their persuasive skills without allowing them to become manipulators.

Try to say "yes" instead of "no" to questions like "Can I pierce my tongue?" "Yes, of course you can, when you are twenty-one and have the experience to make that decision and the money to pay for it."

Orange children learn by experiencing things "hands-on" and need to be taught to think before they act. They need practice in handling anger in acceptable ways, by understanding what causes these reactions. Understand an Orange's putting self in isolation, or taking a time out, is a way to process anger safely.

Their sense of humor, genuine generosity, extreme optimism, and easy sociability are some of their greatest strengths and are important in maintaining high self esteem. These traits should be nurtured to the fullest and recognized by you as positive.

Addressing the Needs of Gold Children

Gold children need a place to be in control. Often having their own room, or even their own section of a room that is designated as "theirs," which they can keep the way they wish, can help them feel in control.

They need to learn that others do not have to be like them, look like them, and act like them—that the world is an interesting place *because* we are all different. There are a number of ways to teach Gold children to appreciate such differences. One successful way is to praise their ability to organize their lives. This skill will lead to success in the long run, and encouraging them early in life emphasizes important traits you will want them to maintain. Also, recognize their kind words, punctuality, and helpfulness in household chores. This recognition can encourage positive behavior between a Gold child and his siblings.

Encourage Gold children's leadership tendencies while emphasizing that good leaders seek advice from others as a way to build bridges in communication. Help them understand that they do not have to be in control of everything at all times. Following is not a bad thing; in fact, it is a skill that is important in learning to relate to others and in good citizenship. Giving control to others can lift a burden from their shoulders, and making mistakes is part of the learning process.

Encourage Gold children to be more flexible by being more flexible as their parent. Take the opportunity to make verbal statements about your flexibility, such as, "I'm proud of myself for being able to change my plans at the last minute without feeling too stressed. I usually have a difficult time with last-minute changes." Golds learn by example.

Teach Gold children to relax with a good book or movie. Teach them that some tasks can wait until tomorrow. "Today we will just stop and smell the roses."

Addressing the Needs of Blue Children

Blue children need an outlet for their emotions. Often drama classes, voice lessons, art lessons or music lessons can provide this outlet, since they love to express themselves in different ways. Encourage their natural artistic abilities.

They often need help in strengthening resolves and boundaries–for example, learning that it is okay to say "no" to things that make them feel uncomfortable rather than giving in and doing what pleases others. They need to learn that although they may be followers, they can make their own decisions, even when those decisions may not be popular. Blue children need to be encouraged to become more leader-like. They need to learn that they have the ability to encourage others.

As a parent of Blue children, praise their giving nature. Nurture their ability to care for others while pointing out that caring for oneself is not selfish but necessary in order to truly give the fullest attention to others. People who are happy with themselves are better friends to others.

Teach Blue children to handle conflict in ways that are acceptable yet comfortable. Teach them to stand up for themselves in a healthy manner. They may need some practice in doing this because it does not come naturally to most Blue children.

Give Blue children opportunities to talk about their feelings. They will tend to ignore those inner feelings if they deem them inappropriate. Teach them that feelings are like facts—neither good nor bad. Feelings simply exist. Feelings are the way our bodies communicate with our minds to help us determine a course of action.

Blue children's genuine concern for others and their ability to put others first are two of their greatest strengths. Their easy going nature makes them likable and should be nurtured and recognized by you, the parent.

Addressing the Needs of Green Children

Green children need to have an outlet for their intellect. Give them "the floor" from time to time and encourage them to share their knowledge. They enjoy competing in games that test their intellectual abilities and analytical skills. They need to understand "rules" before they will abide by them. They need to understand that society is full of rules and they must conform to them at some level in order to live peacefully with people. They need to learn to show compassion to others. Often they are wrapped up in themselves and don't even notice others are present. They have a hard time expressing emotion, but "no man is an island" and Greens must learn that others need to be noticed.

Since Green children are uncomfortable expressing feelings, you should teach them that feelings are our body's way of communicating with our mind in order to formulate a course of action.

Enjoy and praise your Green children's abilities to solve problems with creative ideas, to "think outside the box," and to think things through before making a final decision. Recognize a Green's strong will as an asset in becoming a unique individual. Because Green children tend to be loners, let them know that it is okay to be a follower. And, it is also okay to be a leader, knowing that not everyone will agree with you. Human nature dictates that we are all different.

Green children learn best by self-discovery. The computer can be their best friend because it holds so many answers to so many questions, yet it makes few demands on them socially. Because their brains naturally act as computers, categorizing items, they have an innate ability to understand how computers work and how to get the most out of them. You could, for example, praise your Green child's ability with the computer and ask for clarification on its use (especially if you really need it). This exercise will allow interaction between you both on a level that your Green will feel comfortable.

Green children often have dry wits, and their command of language makes them entertaining when they feel comfortable with their audience. Give them opportunities to express themselves in ways that enhance sociability. Videotaping them is a great way to accomplish this without embarrassing them. Be sure to let them preview themselves.

Chapter 12

STRENGTHENING YOUR LOWEST COLOR

Review the chart below and mark all the STRENGTHS you feel you have in all the colors. Pay particular attention to the list of traits of your lowest color. Which traits (that you did NOT mark) do you feel you can develop or improve? Select at least three wished-for STRENGTHS from the list of your least color.

ORANGE	GOLD	BLUE	GREEN
Independent	Organized	Communicator	Confident
Flexible	Committed	Creative	Self-assured
Works well in crisis	Consistent	Willing to help	Determined
Gets things done	Loyal	Supportive	Patient
Open-minded	Practical	Compassionate	Perseveres
Positive Outlook	Predictable	Tolerant	Logical
Energetic	Responsible	Good Listener	Has Integrity
Confident	Dependable	Enthusiastic	Ambitious
Motivated	Accountable	Loving	Inventive
Fearless	Orderly	Intuitive	Good strategist
Takes charge	Follows through	People-skilled	Has global sense
Humorous	Reliable	Inspirational	Conceptual
Adaptable	Structured	Giving	Analytical
Spontaneous	Law-abiding	Dedicated	Research-oriented
Unafraid of failure	Hard working	Facilitating	Hangs in there!!!

What is your lowest color? ________________________

List three unmarked STRENGTHS from your least color that you would like to develop or improve:

____

____

____

Now, review the next chart and mark all the VALUES you feel you have in all the colors. Again, pay particular attention to the list of traits of your lowest color. Which traits (that you did NOT mark) do you feel you can develop or improve? Select at least three wished-for VALUES from the list of your least color.

ORANGE	GOLD	BLUE	GREEN
Freedom	Loyalty	Honesty	Intellectual achievement
Adventure	Dependability	Friendship	Logic
Independence	Perfection	Children	Knowledge
Spontaneity	Responsibility	Sensitivity	Ideas
Variety	Honesty	Harmony	Learning
Fun/Play	Organization	Compassion	Accomplishment
Flexibility	Consistency	Sharing	Creativity
Risk-taking	Punctuality	Love	Competency
Uniqueness	Integrity	Caring	Freedom
Interaction	Planning	Creativity	Understanding "why"
People's differences	Cleanliness	Spirituality	Integrity
Approval	Justice	Relationships	Original thought
Winning	Truth	Nature	Information
Humor	Family	Music	Anything new
Quick wit	Dedication	Romance	Innovation
Optimism	Being Prepared	Trust	Independence
Just doing it!!	Quality	Optimism	Not looking foolish

What is your lowest color? ________________________

List three unmarked VALUES from your least color that you would like to develop or improve:

____

____

____

Next, review the following chart and mark all the SKILLS you feel you have in all the colors. Once more, pay particular attention to the list of traits of your lowest color. Which traits (that you did NOT mark) do you feel you can develop or improve? Select at least three wished-for SKILLS from the list of your least color.

ORANGE	GOLD	BLUE	GREEN
Producing	Organizing	Guiding	Designing
Repairing	Accounting for	Public Speaking	Inventing
Selling	Guarding	Listening	Analyzing
Competing	Caretaking	Teaching	Problem solving
Public Speaking	Following directions	Recruiting	Orderly thinking
Persuading	Handling details	Counseling	Conceptualizing
Manufacturing	Dispatching	Persuading	Researching
Constructing	Securing	Leading	Developing
Negotiating	Supervising	Motivating	Reasoning
Manipulating	Coordinating	Training	Mapping out
Responding to crises	Collecting data	Mentoring	Diagnosing
Operating Tools	Doing routine work	Working as a team	Intellectualizing

What is your lowest color? ______________________

List three unmarked SKILLS from your least color that you would like to develop or improve:

____

____

____

Getting your needs met

Finally, review the chart below and mark the NEEDS you wish for most. Include all of the colors. Remember you are a spectrum of all four colors. Once you have finished, consider those NEEDS you have marked. Be ready to answer these questions: Do you feel your NEEDS are not being met? *Who* can you ask for help to meet those needs? *How* can you ask for what you NEED?

ORANGE	GOLD	BLUE	GREEN
Freedom	Stability	Harmony	Autonomy
Activity	Loyalty	Love	Quiet
Affirmation	Neatness	Affection	Alone time
Recognition	Cleanliness	Hugs	No interruptions
Attention	Schedules	Smiles	My own "space"
Competition	Security	Acceptance	Solitude
Challenge	Respect	People	Freedom
Fun/Play	Rules	Friends	Answers
Excitement	Procedures	Romantic gestures	Challenges
Stimulation	Appreciation	Honesty	Information
Surprises	Order	Compassion	Intelligence

Independence	Consistency	Intimacy	Perfectionism
Variety	Cooperation	Approval	Mental creativity
Expression	Punctuality	Inspiration	My knowledge appreciated
Opportunity to risk	Others to follow my directions	To be acknowledged for being me	Time to think things out

Who can you ask for help to meet your needs?

____

How will you ask? Write the words that you will use:

____

____

____.

Chapter 13

Same Thing, Different Reasons

We all have similar likes; we all have commonalities in the things we do. But we often differ in our motivations. None of this is wrong, just different!

Money

Orange: "I love to spend money on my friends, myself, and loved ones. I never have enough. I spend whatever I have. I am sure that one day I will win the lottery."

Gold: "Saving money is important to me. I must have a "nest egg" for unforeseen needs. I am comfortable with a large savings account that will take care of my children's education and still leave me with plenty for my old age. I don't want to be dependent on my children. I automatically put money in my savings before I even pay any bills."

Blue: "I'm not really very good at balancing a checkbook. I would prefer to have an allowance and have someone else tend to money problems. I'd rather not know about things related to money. I trust my co-partner to handle finances. I become very stressed if I have to figure out money things. I just want enough to meet my family's needs."

Green: "Money is only important if you don't have enough. I may have several bank accounts, some that I don't even remember opening. It just seemed like a good idea at the time. I don't really worry much about bills and sometimes have to be reminded several times before I can find the time to tend to them. However, I love to research the "market" and, if I have enough money, I like to play my hunches."

Travel

Orange: "I'll go anywhere at anytime; just give me a few minutes to pack."

Gold: "I need to plan very carefully. I want to know I can afford to travel in the style I like. I stick to my budget and would prefer to pay ahead if I can."

Blue: "I love to visit relatives and old friends, but I would much rather have them visit me. I want them to stay with me in my home so that I can pamper them. I do enjoy beautiful scenery, moonlight walks on the beach, watching the sunset over the water, romantic time with the one I love."

Green: "I like to travel to learn about new cultures, but a vacation to me is going to an isolated spot on a mountain or to an island with no phone and no tourists."

Football

Orange: "If I'm not on the field, I want to be close enough to hear the helmets and shoulder pads crash. I definitely prefer to be there live, not to watch on TV, but I am not opposed to a Monday night football party!"

Gold: "I believe organized sports can be entertaining. I like the fact that the rules are always the same, penalties are awarded, and the game goes on."

Blue: "I love to have people come and visit to watch the game. I'm usually too busy preparing food and serving everyone to really notice the game. But that's okay with me. Football can be so brutal sometimes."

Green: “I am into fantasy football. You can choose your own team, trade weekly if research shows another player is doing well. I love to scout the rookies that no one else knows about. I am a keeper of trivia, too. I know more statistics than anyone else and love to predict the winners.”

Cars

Orange: “I want a flashy car that goes really fast.”

Gold: “I want a trustworthy automobile that has been proven to be efficient and long lasting.”

Blue: “I would like a mini van into which all the family can fit comfortably and which can hold all the children for car pool.”

Green: “I research the best deal in Consumers Digest. I know exactly what features I want and what they will cost. I sometimes like to “haggle” with a salesman, but if he talks down to me I will never be back.”

Books, Television and Movies

Orange: “Fast action adventure flicks get my attention.”

Gold: “Give me docu-dramas, Law and Order, things about history, traditional favorites, and the classics.”

Blue: “I like romance novels, self-help books, comedies and sitcoms on TV, movies with happy endings.”

Green: “I want science fiction, mysteries, the weather channel, documentaries on factual things that interest me.”

Chapter 14

KEEPING THEM SAFE

All families can expect trouble in rearing their children. How you handle problems will influence your children for years to come. All children need consistency in order to learn how to make life's tough decisions. They have to learn that there are consequences for their decisions. When subjects such as violence, sex, and drugs come up, consequences must be clearly understood. How, then, can you teach your children to act and react in ways that are appropriate? The answer begins when children are small.

Learning is constant and sequential. From infancy, babies learn that crying gets them fed or changed. They are continually processing your reactions. They learn, for example, that their smile receives a positive reaction from you. As they begin to crawl and get into things, your reactions send messages of approval, concern, and places and things to be avoided. Your aggressive reaction teaches children aggression and fear. Their learning to fear results from their hearing your emphatic "NO!!!" or your threatening words, or a painful slap to the hand or leg. Attempting to control a child through fear teaches him that his self-control is tied to anger and fear. What is the lesson learned by the child? Manipulating through fear and using violence are appropriate behaviors for getting what you want. Ultimately, your children will learn how to handle relationships by the way *you* deal with them.

An alternative: Instead of yelling at or striking your child, try removing him from the conflict with a simple "No," then distract him with a toy or a different positive activity. Soon, your child will learn what toys they can play with and what activities they can do without interruption.

Children look to their parents for lessons in life skills. At the end of a stressful day, do we need to reach for a cocktail or a "nerve pill" or some chemical that will help relieve the stress. Wouldn't you rather find "healthy" ways to handle your stress to be modeled by your children. Sometimes you may use the Orange part of you to cope with stress by doing something physical. Your Gold side relieves stress by prioritizing lists of things to do. The Blue part of you may get lost in a good book or take a bubble bath. Your Green side may find a quiet spot to just think. You can view stress as a catalyst for creativity; deal with it in positive, active ways. When your children see how you handle stress, they are learning lessons. Although children may not seem to hear ninety percent of what you say, they imitate ninety percent of what they see you do.

Children learn respect for the opposite sex by observing their parents. "Off color" comments about the opposite sex send a message of disrespect, even contempt. Silence during sexually suggestive or explicit television or movie scenes can be interpreted as acceptance of what is being depicted. Your children see your reactions and learn. *Your child's* perception of a good sexual relationship is a reflection of the way *you* react to sexual situations. Both the best and the worst lessons are learned at home. No caring parents purposely set unhealthy examples for their children, but they need to remember that every experience is a learning experience for their children and that they as parents are their children's primary teachers.

A variety of factors influence children, many of which the parents are unaware. As a parent, you cannot always know what your children's perception of your actions may be. Neither can you always measure how they are processing other information that comes from the home environment. For example, children are exposed to hundreds of advertisements via television. You might want to pay closer attention to the content. Some advertisements are for pharmaceutical products. What messages are your children digesting from these commercials? –a pill or a powder to cure every ill? If you feel poorly take a drug? Is that the message you want sent to them, or, as their teacher, would you present them a healthier alternative?

One television commercial depicts a young man admiring an expensive sports car. A beautiful woman approaches, showing interest in him, until the real owner of the car appears. When she realizes her mistake, she walks away disgusted. An interesting message for a child! Likewise, a beer commercial shows beautiful, bikini-clad women flocking to young men because they drink the "right" brand of beer.

What do your children process from these ads? Is it that owning the right car gets the beautiful woman? You can get the babe on the beach in the bikini if you drink the right beverage? Sex sells!–even to children. In our culture, this is called good advertising. It gets our attention and entices us to purchase products. Advertising is not all bad, of course, but parents should not assume that it has no impact on young minds.

You might ask yourself: Which has the greater influence on children, parental warnings or children's cartoons? Even in classic cartoons, we can see an elephant getting drunk in order for him to believe he can fly. A cute space creature gets drunk and begins to share feelings with his new earthling friend, who is also drunk. His classmates think he is really funny and cool, and no consequences about the effects of alcohol are suggested.

In movies that are marketed to teens, binge drinking is the norm, and, with few exceptions, these scenes depict how cool it is to get soused. The message of acceptance for underage alcohol use is clear. How many children watch such shows and movies, and are influenced by them? We don't know. But children, infant to adolescent, are learning lessons from each one. A good practice on the way home from movies or after watching a television program is to discuss with your children the scenes that were disturbing to you. Remind young children that movies are not real and do not always depict things accurately. Give factual information on the effects of alcohol on a young, developing brain. State your concerns about what was seen and talk about consequences of behaviors in the real world. Monitor the entertainment your children see. Spend more time with them; play games; teach skills; watch less television.

Everything your children see and hear is interpreted in their minds and stored as "research material." They use this research material to make decisions. When the opportunity presents itself to behave in the way they have seen, their decision will either be yes or no.

For example: A little boy is attending his first school dance. His "research material" tells him it is proper and probably fun to ask a girl to dance. He has seen others do it. His perception that it would be a good thing motivates him to try. He picks out a really cute girl and walks over to her and asks her to dance. She says, "Sure," and they proceed to dance. His confidence level is high so he asks other girls to dance and has a great time. This was a good experience. The experience agreed with his perception of what would happen. The consequence of his action was positive.

What if the opposite had happened? What if the cute little girl laughed at him and said, “No”? Would he have asked another girl to dance? Even though he had seen other couples dancing and it looked like fun, his first experience was not good. His experience did not match his perception. The consequence was negative. Now he may be confused. Dancing looked like fun on television. What happened? This new bit of information is added to his “research” base and he now has a different perception of how fun it is to attend a dance, or ask to a girl to dance, or talk to pretty girls.

If the perception and the experience were good, he is likely to repeat it. If the perception was good and the experience was bad, he is less likely to repeat it. If the perception was bad, the experience may not have even happened.

Our job as parents is to feed information to that “research base” so that healthy events are perceived as positive and unhealthy events are perceived as negative. We can never be assured that our children’s decisions will be what we would have chosen, but at least we can give them information so that their perceptions approach what life really is.

Of course, parents do not know what our children are thinking. Parents cannot know what is going on inside their children’s heads. There is no way to know everything that children have seen or heard, how they have processed the information, or what they have concluded from it. But we sometimes get hints from the way they behave, from the materials they read, from the songs they listen to, from the television programs they enjoy, from the clothes they wear, or from the personal appearance they want. The best indicator of your children’s thoughts may be manifested in their friends. Who are they? What are they like? What do they do for fun? After all, "Birds of a feather flock together." Parents should take the opportunity to praise those things they like in their children's friends and address those things they do not like.

The bottom line is try to communicate with your child through his/her dominant "color," keeping in mind that his/her *complete* color spectrum has a great effect on who he/she is and how he/she acts.

Orange

Some Orange children may be stimulated by the perceived "adventure" of violence, sex, and drugs. They love risky behavior. Probably more than the others, Orange children would benefit by parents limiting TV time and closely monitoring the movies Orange children watch and the video games they play. As a parent of an Orange child, set forth logical consequences for acting out violence. For instance, hitting friends means not being able to play with them for a day or two; breaking toys means they will not be replaced. Consequences must be immediate, but short in duration. If you send your child to his room for a long period, he may use that time to plot revenge. For older Orange children, let them experience the consequences of their actions outside the home. If they get suspended from school, don't come to their defense; if they break something, make them pay to replace it. Orange children may benefit from learning skills in conflict resolution and behavior modification. Most communities have such opportunities for a child to attend formal classes through a youth services agency.

Violence Prevention: Help fill your Orange child's time with active sports like football, soccer, swimming, gymnastics, and track and field. Orange children thrive on learning skills that enable them to use their hands to be creative, such as woodworking, cooking, and mechanics. KEEP THEM BUSY! Reacting physically is natural to Orange children. Teach them to use words rather than fists when angered. They may view their violent actions as a means of control, especially if they have been disciplined with physical actions such as spankings. Teach them to disagree *verbally* and to ask for what they need.

Sex: Orange teenagers are naturally interested in sexual feelings, more so than children of the other primary colors. Assure them that these feelings are normal but don't have to be acted out. Limit their access to television and movies, especially those that are sexual in nature. Monitor relationships with the opposite sex. Be aware of their environment–an empty house is an opportunity for mischief. Provide information about sexual behavior. Explain that consequences are not limited to unwanted pregnancy but can be a matter of life and death. If you don't know what to say, find written material to pass on to your Orange child. Don't assume your child knows. Discuss definitions of good relationships and have your child verbalize what he/she is looking for in a future mate. Stress that sex is a healthy part of marriage but can be both physically and emotionally damaging when it is the only basis for a relationship.

Drugs: Orange children love to feel good! Any substance that alters the way a person feels is a drug. The availability of any drug increases the probability of its use. Today, the most available drug is alcohol, which is *illegal* for anyone under age twenty-one. Some parents of Orange children think, "At least he is only drinking. He is going to do it anyway, and I'd rather have him drinking than doing drugs." Alcohol is a very dangerous substance, especially in an adolescent's bloodstream.

Too often parents say things like, "Just don't drive if you have been drinking," or "Don't drink too much. Just have one or two." Statements such as these give the child permission to drink. Be your child's excuse to say "No" to drugs. Set firm expectations about the NO USES of illegal substances, and follow up with consistent consequences. Provide your children with the words to use, such as "Are you kidding! My Mom will take away my driver's license for life if I drink or use drugs." or "I'll be grounded for two weeks if I do that." Not only does a child lack the experience to make decisions about his/her own sobriety, but also his/her body processes alcohol differently than does an adult's. Physical addiction can happen in a matter of months to young, developing adolescents. Because they are learning social skills, as well, these skills can remain undeveloped when alcohol is used. For example, if a young man can only feel comfortable talking to girls "under the influence," he will have a difficult time developing that confidence without alcohol. An Orange adolescent is impulsive by nature, and alcohol increases that tendency. The combination of Orange and alcohol is deadly. Do not fall into the trap of accepting alcohol use by your Orange children.

Illegal drugs are even more addictive and dangerous than alcohol. Oranges sometimes want to take the "easy way out." Unfortunately, drugs can quickly and easily give Oranges the feelings that they are seeking. There are drugs for a host of feelings. Oranges tend to be polydrug users, meaning that any drug will do. They like experimenting with their feelings. In treatment centers, the majority of Oranges are not there because they want help; rather they were offered treatment in lieu of jail time. Relapse is frequent and swift in Oranges unless there is a genuine desire to quit. When returned to the former environment, Oranges are the most likely of the colors to return to their old friendships and fall back into the cycle of drug use. Oranges certainly can recover, but it is difficult. Long-term treatment and aftercare are often necessary.

Of all the colors, Oranges are at highest risk for unhealthy behaviors, and parental prevention and intervention are extremely important. Review the needs of the Orange children in your family and do everything to stay on top of their behaviors. Interventions must be swift and your actions consistent. For Oranges, freedom must be earned by responsible behavior. Strive to steer your Orange children on paths that enhance their strengths, and remember: KEEP THEM BUSY!

Gold

Gold children are motivated by control. They love the feeling of being in control, not only of themselves, but of other people and situations. Although they have a strong sense of right and wrong, their perceptions can be influenced by other people and what they see on television in the movies.

Violence prevention: As a parent of Gold children, monitor what they see in the media. Verbalize your objections to questionable scenes that depict violent control issues. For young people today, the popular movies depict heroes who rule by violence–shootings, bombings, murders. If violence as the means of control is perceived as proper, your Gold children may act on it.

Early on, set logical consequences for acts of violence. When Gold children use violence to control their friends, don't allow them to play with them for a day or two. Express your displeasure. Teach them to use words, not actions, to express desires. Gold children love options. Give them choices of ways to deal with disagreements that include compromise. Golds like to follow the rules, but they have to know what the rules are. TELL THEM.

Sex: If Gold children have seen sex used to control, they may perceive this as normal behavior. Take time to discuss with your children what a good relationship is, and have them verbalize what they want in a future mate. Talk about plans for marriage and family. Gold children love to plan their future, and creating time lines in adolescence allows Gold children to form a picture of what their lives can be. Discuss those things that might hinder their success, such as unwanted pregnancy. Information about Sexually Transmitted Diseases (STD) can be a deterrent, especially for Golds.

Drugs: Alcohol use is pervasive among teens in today's society, even among Golds. Two deterrents for Gold children are the illegality and the expense of alcohol. But be aware that children will raid their parents' liquor cabinets to reduce the expense. The Gold child is least likely to experience trouble with alcohol or other drugs, but the allure of peers can be difficult to overcome. If drinking appears to be the popular thing, any child can be persuaded to participate. Illegal drug use by Golds is uncommon but possible. If Gold overachievers discover that "speed" gives them the energy to produce at a higher level, they may fall prey. Information on the realities of drug use is essential. Although Golds are achievers and prefer to feel in control of their actions, which results in low drug use among this group, don't be lulled into a false sense of security. If you suspect drug use, confront them. Golds will accept treatment when they realize that their drug use is interfering with their achievement.

Blue

Blue children are motivated by acceptance of others. During adolescence they are particularly vulnerable to peer groups. Being more naturally followers than leaders, Blue children should have their friendships monitored by you, their parent. You may be more aware of "trouble" in *other* children and thus able to spot it in your own child.

Violence prevention: Because Blue children are harmonious and loving, they are unlikely to act out in any violent way. However, if Blues feel cornered, they may come out swinging. If and when they do, they usually respond well to reprimand. Remind them to use words, not fists. Blues love to express themselves verbally and are often very dramatic. Any violence is usually aimed at themselves, which can be a danger for Blue children. Because they are so emotional, they sometimes behave irrationally. A parent's challenge is to teach them skills to divide emotion from reality. Take time to truly listen to your Blue children, especially when they seem upset or depressed. Teach them to keep a journal of their feelings so that when they are despondent they remind themselves how they relieved similar past difficulties. If your Blue children perceive that violence is acceptable in a relationship, they may accept personal abuse. Monitor the movies and television they watch and discuss those scenes that are disturbing to you. Violence is never acceptable. No one ever deserves to be battered. Your Blue child is far more likely to be the recipient of violence than the instigator.

Sex: Blue children are vulnerable to involvement in a sexual relationship. Because they want to love and be loved they may become sexually involved early on. Blues often confuse sex with love. As the parent of Blue children, have them verbalize their dreams for love and marriage and discuss what they are looking for in a permanent mate. Stress that sex is a healthy part of marriage but can be physically and emotionally damaging when it is the only basis for a relationship. Limit access to television and movies that have strong sexual content. Closely monitor your children's relationships. Encourage group dating and minimize long periods of unsupervised "one-on-one" time. Provide information on STDs and stress that unprotected sex is a matter of life and death, not just unwanted pregnancy. Tell them that sex is not a way to "prove you love me."

Drugs: Because Blues are followers, they will go along with the crowd. The use of alcohol and other drugs will be linked to their feeling accepted. Their drug of choice may be marijuana or some other depressant, or a hallucinogenic like ecstasy, since Blues prefer the "mellow" feeling. Blues will enter treatment programs if someone else asks them. They hate to disappoint the ones they love. In-patient treatment is difficult for Blues because they hate to be away from their home and their loved ones. Once they connect with a counselor or other recovering people, the task becomes easier and a way to make new friends.

Green

Increased knowledge and self-discovery motivate Green children. They thrive on experiencing things before anyone else. They use their intellect and cleverness as social tools.

Violence Prevention: Green children are rarely physically violent. They are more likely to use their intellect to compete in non-aggressive battles. Their internal struggles are often overlooked because they are so quiet. Because Greens are loners and usually not involved in many extracurricular activities, it may be more difficult for them to identify and verbalize strong feelings that they are experiencing. Keep open the lines of communication with your Green children. Have them help you prepare dinner or plan and plant gardens. They are more comfortable one on one. Make special time to be with them. Green children love projects. Become actively interested and involved in your children's projects. At four years old, they love to help prepare dinner; at eight, they love to research dinosaurs or collect bugs; in teenage years, they love to design buildings, houses, the "perfect" city. Greens love being "smarter" than you are. Give them opportunities to "show off" their skills.

Sex: Green's natural curiosity and need to experience and experiment may lead to sexual activity. However, since they are usually introverted they may have trouble with dating. More than likely, they will become involved with someone who seeks them out. As a parent of Green children, provide them with information about sexual issues. You may find that they have trouble discussing sex, so written material may help. Or, you may find that they may already know more than you think. At any rate, don't assume they know. Provide the information.

Parents of Green children sometimes are afflicted with the false worry that their Green children are not socially active. It is within their nature and comfort level to have just a few friends and spend a lot of time alone. Encourage their friendships but do not force social activity. They may prefer to be with a few friends to attending a crowded dance or party.

Green children are often musically inclined. This is a wonderful outlet for energy and emotion. Much can be learned about thoughts and feelings by listening to lyrics and musical tones. Music can become a comfortable way to be social.

Drugs: Green children may not be quite as enamored by alcohol as children of other colors, primarily because alcohol dulls the mind. Greens are usually smart enough to realize that using alcohol or other drugs may interfere with their ability to succeed. However, their innate need to experiment places them at some risk. Mind-expanding drugs like XTC and other acids may be alluring to Greens if they perceive that there is no danger. Provide your Green children with information on the dangers of drugs. Focus especially on the long-range damage to the brain. Impress upon them that brain damage is permanent and will interfere with their ability to attain knowledge and retrieve it easily.

Help is Available–Use it Early

Your children are your most valuable assets. Because you love them, it is easy to overlook danger signs. It is also easier to make excuses for them than to acknowledge their problems and take action. Early intervention is the key to successfully eliminating problems. If you suspect a problem in any of these areas - violence, sex, or drugs - confront your child with your concerns and seek professional assistance. Help is available through local youth services agencies, school systems, and drug treatment programs. There are also numerous ALANON groups that help families of drug users to cope and become educated.

Seek out parenting education classes in your community. Taking a parenting class is an opportunity to learn to communicate better with your family members. Your children are in your home for a limited number of years. Enjoy them and cherish those years. Do everything possible to create wonderful memories. Give your children roots which will provide them stability and wings so that they become productive adults. Be their excuse to say “No” to unhealthy activities.

Contracts

Use contracts to negotiate behaviors that you expect from your children. Contracts work well because the expectation is set in writing for all parties to see. An added benefit is that they begin to understand the importance of legal agreements. It is best to make the contract before problems start so it is not used as a punishment but as a preventive measure. Treating children with respect earns their respect.

Here are some possible contracts:

I, ___________________, will bring home my friends and introduce them to my parents for the privilege of using the car one night each weekend until 10:30. I understand that any use of alcohol or other drugs will negate this contract.

_______________________ ____________________________

Child’s name / Parent’s name

I, ________________, will perform the duties and responsibilities listed below, in a timely manner, for the privilege of extending curfew until 11:30 on Saturday nights. Duties and responsibilities:

Maintain my grades (state specific level, i.e. A, B, C average)

Keep my room neat (be specific—put away clothes, vacuum, make bed)

Use appropriate language (no cursing)

Put garbage at curbside on Tuesdays and Fridays

_______________________ ____________________________

Child’s name / Parent’s name

Contracts should be simple and focus on one specific reward. If your child does not respond to verbal agreements, you may have several written contracts going at the same time. Contracts are always open for renegotiations by both parties.

The Dreaded Driver's License

The age of attaining a legal driver's license is a legal limit, not a mandate. This means that a child ***may, if the parents deem it acceptable***, receive a driver's license. Driving is a privilege, not a right! It is earned by showing responsibility. Putting a child behind the wheel of a heavy expensive lethal *weapon* before he demonstrates skill and responsibility is asking for trouble. I suggest some questions and guidelines before you offer this privilege:

Does your child realize the importance of this event?

Can your child afford the expense of this privilege?
(insurance, gas, maintenance)

Does your child understand the seriousness involved in driving a vehicle? (Cars can kill–more teenagers are killed in automobile accidents than any other cause, and often alcohol is involved.)

Do you have rules about the use of the car? Here are suggestions:

No driving at night for at least six months.

No driving with more than two friends in the car for one year.

No driving with cell phone in the "on" position.

Driver pays for gasoline and other related expenses.

Driver pays for insurance (or a portion).

Driver pays for all tickets received and faces family penalty as well (to be determined by severity of offense).

Driver pays for any damage done to the vehicle and faces losing the use of it (to be determined by severity of circumstance).

Any automobile for exclusive use of the teen driver will be paid for (or a portion thereof) and maintained by said driver.

The driver's license becomes your teenager's most coveted possession. However, to restate, obtaining and using the license is a *privilege*, not a *right.* Withdrawing this privilege should be at the parents' discretion. This is a important piece of paper and should not be taken lightly. It is a symbol of freedom; freedom is earned; too much freedom given quickly (simply because one has a birthday) can be a problem.

Teens are easily distracted. Fiddling with the radio, talking on a cellular phone, laughing with friends, eating a hamburger, drinking a cola, lighting a cigarette, glancing at someone walking down the street, or watching a cute "someone" in the rear view mirror are all dangerous. Too many young drivers are injured or killed in car crashes that would not have happened to a more experienced driver.

Encourage your teen drivers to practice, practice, practice. Of course, this means *you* will be spending time with them in the car to insure that the practicing is done. This can be a wonderful experience for you both. Before your child ever applies for his Learner's Permit, sit down and discuss expectations, make agreements, and coordinate schedules. This is a time when you will have to learn to let go. With a driver's license comes the independence that your teen will not have experienced before. This can be a stressful time for you both.

The driving privilege should be gradually earned, not just handed out based on age or eligibility definitions in the law.

The process of driver education, obtaining a license, practicing, and establishing guidelines may be one of your last opportunities to spend quality time teaching your child skills that he will use the rest of his life. What a perk if he suddenly realized that others of your lessons were worthwhile, too!

Chapter 15

Learning Styles, Wants, Needs, Rewards, Consequences

It is important to understand that we learn in different ways, according to our "colors." Education has spent many years training teachers to incorporate all 4 learning styles in their class instruction.

Oranges are experiential learners. They need hands-on activities.
Golds are didactic learners. They can read and follow directions.
Blues are cooperative learners. They want to discuss with others.
Greens are self-discoverers. They would prefer to be left alone to figure things out.

Choices and consequences

There are things that children want and there are things children need. You cannot withhold their needs—safety, food, shelter, recognition, love, belonging, and self-expression. To differentiate, make a list of the things your children want, such as: toys, money, freedom, clothes, TV time, use of the car, telephone. Make this list long and specific. To reward your children for fulfilling their responsibilities, choose from the Wants list. To discipline, take something away from the Wants list.

You can make a chart to demonstrate to your children exactly how this works:

Responsibility	Reward	Consequence
Put toys away	Toys for birthday	Remove some toys
Take care of clothes	Those jeans you want	No new clothes

Whenever possible, relate the consequence to the responsibility. For example: If your son is not taking care of his toys, remove some of them until he has earned them back by caring for the remaining ones. If he is taking good care of his toys, get him one on his Wants list for his birthday. If your teenage daughter is late for curfew, reduce her freedom by thirty minutes the next time she is out. Again, she can earn back those minutes through abiding by the rules.

Oranges and Greens will benefit from knowing exactly what the consequences are. They still may decide that a consequence is worth it, and they may try to change the rules frequently.

Golds will love the structure and equality of the whole concept. They will love to distribute weekly job charts and to be fair about taking turns with the yucky jobs. Blues will enjoy getting their instructions and receiving their rewards.

Remember to tell *all* your children exactly what you expect. Be specific about their jobs. You will often need to *show* them how to do something; don't just expect them to know what you want. Golds and Blues will be willing to learn; Golds will learn faster. Oranges and Greens may resist, and Greens will learn faster.

Family norms are those things that are expected of all family members. Like your family mission statement, norms consist of what the *family* believes in. They consist of what the expected behavior is for everyone. Some examples are:

Treat each other with respect. No swearing. No name calling. No shouting. No hitting.

Listen to the heart as well as the words—if someone needs a hug, give them one. Be loyal to the family—don't gossip or tell tales that may be embarrassing. Stick together—protect each other outside as well as inside the home. Family norms are for everyone!

Mother's Responsibilities

Responsibility	Reward	Consequence

Father's Responsibilities

Responsibility	Reward	Consequence

CHILD'S RESPONSIBILITIES

_____________ (Child's Name)

Responsibility Reward Consequence

CHILD'S RESPONSIBILITIES

_____________ (Child's Name)

Responsibility Reward Consequence

Child's Responsibilities

______________ (Child's Name)

Responsibility	Reward	Consequence

Child's Responsibilities

______________ (Child's Name)

Responsibility	Reward	Consequence

Chapter 16

Activities for Families

Strengthen the family unit. A strong, healthy family has strong, healthy children who become strong, healthy citizens that create a strong, healthy community. To state the obvious: family activities are important to children. Sometimes we get so busy that we all just exist in the same house. It is important to stop, take a step back, and look at what's going on in the home. Sometimes we even have to *plan* to make things happen. Try some of these exercises for family time.

Family Structure

The core principle for any organized group, from Scouts to Junior League to the United States of America, is "norms." These norms are printed in the by-laws, charters, articles of incorporation, or the Constitution of the United States. Without norms we would not know what is expected of us. Norms set guidelines for us to follow and define sanctions when guidelines are not met. We will look at three suggested family documents and their possible norms, which set standards about who we are, where we want to go, and how we are going to get there.

Family Mission Statement
Family Job Descriptions
Individual Responsibilities

Family Mission Statement

Who we are: A family mission statement tells something about the beliefs and goals of the family. It is brief, broad, and general in scope, but it sets the tone for family policies.

Example: "The HAYWARDS believe that each family member is important. We treat each other with respect. We communicate our wants, needs, and fears in order to gain support from each other. We believe in helping each other to become the best people we can be. We are a special family who will stand up for one another till the end. ALL FOR ONE AND ONE FOR ALL."

To expand on this concept, you can design a family crest with symbols that have meaning to your family. Trace your family tree and learn about your heritage. Create the idea that your family is unique; there is no other family quite like yours. This gives your children a sense of belonging. They develop a feeling of self-worth and a desire to remain in good standing with the family. This will really come in handy when they are called upon to make decisions outside of the family. They will ask themselves, "What would my family think?"

Getting to Know You

Too often we really don't know who we are or what we are supposed to be doing. Some suggestions: Define family roles. Write job descriptions. Include ALL family members. What are the expectations of MOTHER, FATHER, CHILD? Have *each* family member contribute ideas for *all* job descriptions (i.e. mother write for mother, father, and child; father write for mother, father, and child; child write for mother, father, and child). Once you have all the job descriptions written and collected, review them together and decide, as a family, which ones you all agree on. You can do this sitting around a table with someone taking notes, adding and eliminating as the discussion progresses.

Job descriptions can be fairly general:

Mother—Take care of the children; prepare meals; provide rides to school; do the laundry.

Father–Earn the money; spend "fun time" with the children; take care of the lawn: handle home maintenance.

Child—Attend school and maintain good grades; be respectful to parents and siblings; clean your room.

Family Dog—Love everyone unconditionally; play outside; guard the family.

You may be amazed when you read what others in your family think you should be doing. The expectations for mother may include suggestions from her children that she does not see as her job. Her child's list of her responsibilities could include: "clean my room; help with my school projects; keep cookies available at all times; let me go to bed when I want; not hassle me about my grades." This activity can be a real eyeopener and can identify the source of problems.

Although it is important to get feedback from your children, you are still the parents. Creating job descriptions is a good opportunity to discuss what you, as parents, will accept as your responsibilities and those that you feel belong to others. The process is as important as the end result. Of course, these are just general guidelines for family members. The next step is to set up some specifics. Orange, Gold, Blue, and Green will like this exercise as long as they know they have a voice in all job descriptions. Oranges will want to do the exercise very quickly; Green will want to think it through; Gold will prioritize the list and try to make it equal for all; and Blue will approach it from the point-of-view of personal relations. Golds will like this exercise best and embrace it because it provides family structure.

Write your FAMILY MISSION STATEMENT

Write MOTHER'S JOB DESCRIPTION

Write FATHER'S JOB DESCRIPTION

Write CHILD(REN)'S JOB DESCRIPTION

Write OTHER FAMILY MEMBER'S JOB DESCRIPTION

Family Belief System

With input from your children, create your own family's belief system or, in other words, the rules, norms, choices, responsibilities. Once these norms are written down post them somewhere.

Blue and Gold children will welcome this exercise. They are most comfortable when they know what is expected of them. Green and Orange children *must* be in on the process or they will not abide by the decisions: "Don't tell me what to do!" Let them have a voice in making the norms.

Ground rules: Ask for suggestions from all family members. Let children write down expectations for parents, too. (For example, if your children have a curfew, perhaps you should have one too). Write down *all* suggestions–even if some are unacceptable to you, write them down. In this way, you show respect for the process.

Discuss as a group: Hear each person's opinions as to why this or that rule is important.

Prioritize: In order of importance, list what was voted on by the family. The final list need not be long. In fact, depending on the age(s) of your children, the list may include only three to five norms. A short list for a stated length of time is important if the family is experiencing a crisis. Let the children know the family can revisit these norms.

Be very specific: For example, "Clean your room" can mean different things to different people, especially considering age and gender. You should specify what you mean by "Clean your room." For instance, you could specify, "Put shoes in closet, hang up clothes, put toys on shelves, put school books on the desk, put dirty clothes in the laundry basket." This list can always be revisited, but parents get the final say-so.

Your lists might look something like this:

Mother: (This list could go on forever, but it is not a bad idea to let your children know how much you really do.

Prepare breakfast.

Clean kitchen: wash and put away dishes. Put all food away. Sweep floor.

Car pool—don't forget to send the children off with a kiss and a word of encouragement. Clean the house—vacuum floors; clean parents' room; clean the common rooms: den, living room, dining room. (If children are under 5, include their rooms as well, then modify responsibilities as children get older.)

Do the laundry—wash, dry, fold, iron, put clothes away.

Do errands—groceries, dry cleaners, pharmacy, etc.

Pick up kids from school.

Prepare snacks.

Help with homework.

Prepare dinner—set the table, cook food, serve food, help clear the table, wash dishes, pots and pans, clean the kitchen, put everything away.

OKAY, YOU GET THE PICTURE. This is not an opportunity for Mom to become a martyr, but to let everyone know that she has many responsibilities. Mothers do them because it is their job.

Father:

Help with breakfast.

Kiss the wife and kids goodbye.

Go off to work.

Make workday schedule–(list your responsibilities at work).

Pick up any needed items on the way home
(milk bread, etc.).
Put work clothes away.
Bag up all trash cans and put garbage out.
Repair things as needed around the house.
On weekends, cut the grass, trim the bushes, wash the
car, etc.
Take kids to Little League (coach, taxi, cheerleader).

Again, list all the things you do to make the family run smoothly.

Child: Age should be appropriate! A two-year-old cannot make up his bed, but a four-year-old can do it with your help. Job charts are great for younger children. Use a sticker or check mark as rewards to designate completed assignments.

Job Chart for Little Children

Time Job
7:30 Wake up.
7:45 Go to the potty. Brush your teeth
8:00 Get dressed. Put away pajamas.
8:00 Eat breakfast.
8:30 Play.
11:30 Put toys away. Wash hands.
Noon Eat lunch.
12:30 Take nap.
3:00 Play.
5:00 Put toys away. Wash hands.
5:30 Eat dinner.
7:00 Have bath. Brush teeth.
8:00 Go to the potty. Go to bed.

Job chart for children, ages 6-10

Pick up toys–Put them on the shelf. (You can start this with children as young as two years old, but *you* need to show them how to do the tasks by working alongside them every day for several years.)

Pick up clothes–Put dirty clothes in laundry basket. Put clean clothes in drawers or hang them up. Put shoes in closet.

Do homework.

Help set the table, clear the table, put dishes in dishwasher.

Bathe. Brush teeth.

Watch television–(My suggestion is that you carefully screen what your child watches, and then let them watch on a limited basis. They need to earn this privilege. Allowance can be one or two television hours a day.

Job chart for children, ages 10-14

Tidy room–Put all clothes and shoes in closet. Put schoolbooks on desk. Vacuum once a week.

Do homework–(Schedule time and place.)

Eat dinner with the family.

Enjoy leisure time— (Again, with television, screen carefully what they are watching. Limit time allowed. Encourage reading, computer [limited], writing in a journal, communication, games.

Go to bed. No arguments. ("You may have *in-your-room* time and *lights-out* time.")

Do no hit–not anyone, anywhere! No spitting. No name-calling.

Help with garbage, yard work, cooking. (Find small tasks—age appropriate—to increase your children's responsibilities around the house. Not that you should hand off all your jobs, but teach life skills: cooking, cleaning, gardening, car washing, etc.)

Job chart for children, ages 15-18

Clean your room—(Be specific.)

Do homework—(Schedule time and place.)

Eat dinner with the family.

Enjoy leisure time–(TV, telephone, computer, writing, etc.)

Obey curfew–be home by dinner on weekdays. On weekends suit curfew to age. (At fifteen, 11:00 probably is late enough; at seventeen, midnight or whatever you choose.)

These are only suggestions to get you started. Only you know what you want in your home. Some things to keep in mind: Golds and Greens like to make job charts and keep track of who is doing what. Blues like to see that they are fulfilling their responsibilities and are important to their family. Oranges need to be able to visualize the structure and be reminded of their responsibilities.

Family Traditions

Every family has traditions. Write down your family's traditions so you all can remember how special they are. Tradition is so important for Golds. It represents continuity and family history. Blues enjoy the knowledge of what was and what is to be. Oranges love celebrations. Greens love to invent new traditions.

Traditions can be anything from what your family has done regularly to what has carried over from parents and grandparents. Traditions are things and events you can count on. Traditions make families unique.

Some examples are:

Sunday dinner is always fried chicken, mashed potatoes, and green beans.

For Thanksgiving, we always have turkey, sweet potatoes, dressing, and cranberry sauce.

Mom always wears a witch hat for Halloween.

We always have balloons for birthday parties.

Everyone gets a ten-dollar bill for birthdays.

Nightly sharing at the dinner table—things family members learned today, something good that happened.

Wear green on Tuesdays.

Think about your traditions. What are they? Why are they important to you? Ask your family what traditions are their favorites. Make up new traditions that cater to the needs of your children, remembering their "colors."

Orange children need excitement, adventure, challenge, celebration, movement. The traditions that they like may include vacations, birthday celebrations, good-grade celebrations, *you-got-your-room-cleaned-today!* celebrations, *today-is-Wednesday!* celebrations.

Gold children need stability, sameness, repetition, structure. They enjoy all holiday traditions and traditions that celebrate recognition for a job well done.

Blue children need attention, to feel honored, and the personal touch. They enjoy breakfast in bed for their birthday, a round of applause for a good grade, your sharing their joy at the dinner table.

Green children need recognition for achievement, to be heard and understood. The traditions they like may include sitting at the head of the table for good grades, scheduled time for the parents' undivided attention.

Be creative. Think "outside the box" to create special moments and memories for your family.

List your family's traditions:

Holidays:

____

____

____

____

____

____

____

____

____

____

____

Special days:

____

____

____

____

____

____

____

____

____

____

____

Weekly:

Daily:

Mirror Image

Children are a reflection of their parents and how their parents see them. When children know you feel good about them, they feel good about themselves. Be sure to accentuate the positive things about each child.

Here are some tips that may be helpful:

Orange children

Praise their resourcefulness in getting things done.

Notice their enthusiasm for a subject or task, and help them remain motivated.

Recognize their courage in trying new things.

Gold children

Praise their organizational skills.

Notice their neatness in schoolwork.

Recognize their commitment to completing tasks.

Blue children

Praise their compassion for others.

Notice their thoughtfulness.

Recognize their struggles to make everyone happy.

Green children

Praise their accomplishments.

Notice their tenacity in taking on a task.

Recognize their need for knowledge.

For all children

Praise their efforts to do things for themselves, even if the efforts were not done quite right. Let them know you are proud of them for trying.

Notice their struggle to accomplish things that *they* think *they* should be able to do.

Recognize their ability to bounce back after disappointment.

Respect your child just as you would expect your child to respect you by saying “please,” “thank you,” “excuse me,” and “I’m sorry.” Children learn by imitation.

Show appreciation for your child’s work, whether at school, at home, on the ball field, or in the neighborhood.

Dinner Conversation Starters

Dinner table exercises can create great conversation. Ask each person (parents too) to take turns telling something that happened to them that day. You can acknowledge and celebrate their “colors” by honoring one color each day with questions geared to their temperaments. Some ideas:

To Orange: “What was the most *exciting* thing that happened to you today?”

To Gold: “What was the most *rewarding* thing that happened to you today?”

To Blue: “What do you *admire* most in such-and-such a person?”

To Green: “What did you learn today?”

Train your children to look for exciting and rewarding things—traits that they admire in other people, for example—and have them make note of something new every day. One of the greatest gifts we can give our children is to help them to live life to the fullest every day.

Journals

Encourage everyone to keep personal journals. Some have themes like: Things I am thankful for; Lessons I have learned; My special relationships; My accomplishments. Some journals are used as diaries to record events in everyday life. Whatever type of journal you or your child chooses is worthwhile. Record your history! Celebrate your life! It is great fun to read the things that were important to you even two years ago and to see how you have grown.

Orange: Who knows? You may be famous one day and need to write your autobiography!

Gold: You may want your grandchildren to know their family history.

Blue: This is a place for all you memories and mementos.

Green: You may need to refer back to original ideas that you can perfect later.

Whatever your motivation, JUST DO IT!

To take journal-keeping a step further, create personal albums. Use photographs with narration about what was happening. Children can cut out pictures from magazines showing things they like to do, clothes they like; or styles they want to remember. List songs that are important to you or your children. Include heroes and friends. These are books of memories that they can take with them to college and into adulthood.

The Tree of Dreams

Have each child create a tree that represents a time line of his wishes and dreams. The roots represent birth and first memories, often things that no one knows about. As the tree grows, so do the activities in the child's life. Branches represent milestones in his life—a branch for each school year, for example, with leaves that list friends, events, recognition certificates. Continue up the tree with dreams for the future. Leave enough room for the tree to continue to grow, spaces to add branches as the child adds more dreams. *This tree represents a life's plan. Often we don't plan to fail, we just fail to plan.*

Oranges love permission to dream. Their tree can teach them to think toward the future and make specific plans.

Golds love the continuity of looking *through* their lives, both past and future, and having a plan.

Greens enjoy projecting themselves into the future, one that can be modified at their whim.

Blues love the fantasy of what could be. To write down their dreams and create their future can be very rewarding.

When you as parents participate by making your own Tree of Dreams, you are creating your history for your children. You show them that life is full of ups and downs. You might include some leaves that you wish would *fall off*!—mistakes you made or things that you wish you could do over again. Create some branches that express things you would change–better grades, being kinder to a classmate, taking a job more seriously, continuing your education. Add new branches at the top to include your dreams—taking that trip around the world, writing a novel, getting a college degree, painting a mural, running a marathon, sleeping in for a change. Your children will develop a stronger sense of who you are, a stronger connection to you, and a solid bind to the family you created.

Count Your Blessings!

Be creative! Have everyone keep an ongoing list of blessings. You can write your blessings in a notebook, in your journal, or you can post a list on your bedroom wall. You can add to it each day. These blessings can be anything from small to large:

"I am thankful that we had hamburgers for dinner."

"I am thankful that Grandpa did not die from his heart attack."

List everything you can think of. Have all the family members contribute. Make it a competition! Pick a night to review each member's list—the one with the most blessings listed gets to choose the television program that night. You read them at the dinner table or at a special family time. Or you can post them so that everyone can read them together. These lists can go on and on. There are so many things every day that we can be thankful for. This exercise points out to even the most pessimistic child that life is good!

Same, But Different

Have a bowl of oranges or lemons on the table. Ask each person to choose one and look it over carefully. Then put the fruit back in the bowl, mix them all up, and ask each person to find his fruit. Questions:

How do you know which one is yours? What are the characteristics that stand out?

How is your fruit the same as the others? How is it different?

How does this apply to people?

How does this idea apply to our family?

What are good things about being the same?

What are good things about being different?

Pass the Baton

Choose an item—a stick, a stuffed animal, a ball, something that can be passed around easily. Each person will take a turn to talk as long as he is holding the item—he has the floor with no interruptions, no questions. The person holding the item must relate:

Something great that happened to him this week (month, year, lifetime). Or,

Something that he wishes he could do differently. Or,

Something he admires about someone else in the room. Or,

Someone he would like to meet or be like. Or,

One thing he likes about his family, Or,

One of his best memories about his family.

The Rainbow Connection

No matter what "color" you are, you can learn the traits of all the colors and practice them with your family. Some examples:

Practice being Orange: Believe in yourself by developing a healthy self-image and the ability to cope with setbacks without giving up, by knowing that just because things did not work out this time doesn't mean that they will never work out. There is always *Plan B*. Practice being Orange by trying new things, by being spontaneous with new people and new ideas, by knowing that if you don't take advantage of an opportunity, it may never come around again.

Practice being Gold: Be independent and responsible by teaching your child to do things for himself and accepting responsibility for his part in making the family run smoothly, by learning that his giving his word means *it will get done*. Practice being Gold by respecting authority and others, by practicing knowing the difference between right and wrong, by learning to control yourself, by being courteous, considerate, and fair to others.

Practice being Blue: Accept and love by accepting your child for who he is, all his strengths and challenges, by helping your child understand *that you care anyway,* and by helping your child recognize his "Good"ness. Practice being Blue by giving of yourself , by being generous with yourself and others, by allowing your child to give of himself, his time, his gifts, even if it puts you out.

Practice being Green: Develop a desire for learning by seeking knowledge and answers, by asking questions, by exploring, experimenting, researching, by knowing the value of education. Practice being Green by developing an appreciation for solitude, by being comfortable alone, by taking time to process today's lessons in peace and quiet, by taking time to think things through before making final decisions.

Celebrate!

Create a day to celebrate each of the colors of your family's members.

Celebrate being Orange.

On this day, everyone in the family is Orange. Suggested activities:

1. Sleep in.
2. Eat cake for breakfast. Or eat in the living room or in front of the television set.
3. Take a walk; enjoy the outdoors.
4. Race someone home; the winner gets his choice of food for lunch.

5. Eat out—hot dogs or hamburgers, with ice cream for dessert.
6. Play games.
7. Hand wrestle.
8. Thumb wrestle.
9. Turn on the music—LOUD—and dance.
10. Tell jokes.
11. Throw a party.
12. Wear whatever you want.
13. Go swimming in the winter at a local motel with indoor pool.
14. Leave your bed unmade all day long.
15. Wear different-colored socks.
16. Eat dessert first.
17. Stay up really late.
18. Camp out and tell scary stories.

Celebrate being Gold.

On this day, everyone in the family is Gold. Suggested activities:

1. Eat a big breakfast together. Everyone helps clean up.
2. Make a list of things to do today.
3. Work in the yard together; plant flowers to make it look pretty.
4. After cleaning up, get ready for lunch. Take a vote on where we should go.
5. Read the newspaper and look for coupons or sales.
6. Visit a local department store for time-saving merchandise to make: bins for storage, drawer organizers, files for school papers, calendars, a tablet to keep by the phone for messages.

7. Get a haircut and manicure.
8. Take time to relax.
9. Organize your room using the new organizers.
10. Watch a movie; make popcorn.
11. Reminisce about years gone by.
12. Call family and friends whom you haven't talked to in a while.
13. Make plans for a family vacation.
14. Write in your journal.
15. Everyone eat around the table and have an upbeat conversation.
16. Everyone help clean the kitchen, again, and close it up for the night.
17. Perform night-time rituals: take a bath, brush your teeth, read a book, set your alarm, say good night to everybody, go to bed.

Celebrate being Green.

On this day, everyone in the family is Green. Suggested activities:

1. Get up whenever you want.
2. Eat whatever you want for breakfast, wherever you want.
3. Spend some alone time in your room thinking about what you could do today.
4. Read a book.
5. Use the computer to play games or look up subjects of interest.
6. Explore some new place—a park, forest, library, book store.
7. Play games—Trivial Pursuit, Jeopardy, cards, chess, Scrabble, Clever Endeavor.

8. Create a new dish for lunch or dinner, using whatever is in the kitchen.
9. Discuss topics of interest at the dinner table–space travel, an interesting book, thoughts about what happened to dinosaurs.
10. Design your dream house.
11. Think of places you would like to visit some day.
12. Read some more.
13. Enjoy quiet time to just think, time in which you do not have to share your thoughts with anyone.
14. Go to bed whenever you want.

Celebrate being Blue.

On this day, everyone in the family is Blue. Some suggestions:

1. Be awakened with a hug and a kiss.
2. Share breakfast with everyone at the table or have breakfast in bed.
3. Write a nice note to each family member telling why you think they are special.
4. Talk to friends on the phone.
5. Have friends over to visit.
6. Have a picnic in the park.
7. Eat ice cream cones.
8. Play games—Pictionary, Charades, Monopoly.
9. Make a jigsaw puzzle.
10. Look at family albums.
11. Write in your journal.
12. Create personal gifts for family members.
13. If you are a child, play with old toys.

14. If you are a child, sit in your parents' laps and have them tell you stories.
15. Play soothing music or sing songs.
16. Get a massage.
17. Hold hands with someone you love.
18. Kiss everyone good night.

Celebrate and honor each other for the gifts you all give to your family. Each of you is one of a kind. The ability to understand your own differences, and those of the ones you love, can only enhance your relationships and your future. Your job as parent is to encourage your children to be the best they can be. You cannot mold them into a false hope; you can only guide them to become their best selves.

Being a parent is the most important job you will ever have, and probably the most difficult. Ann Landers said, "In the final analysis, it is not what *you* do for your children but what you have taught *them* to do for themselves that will make them successful human beings."

I wish you luck and love with your children. Remember: none of us is perfect. Accept each other despite your differences. It is because of these differences that the world is a wonderful place to live.

"Once our children of any age understand and accept who they are, not who someone else thinks they should be, they will find the journey to happiness, success and contentment far less difficult. Positive esteem is built while flying our true colors."

—Don Lowry, founder of True Colors

References

Joseph Sullivan and Fred Leafgren, *Personality Effectiveness Workbook* (Personality Resources International,1999).

Don Lowry, *Building Esteem with Your Family* (True Colors, Inc., 1990).

Don Lowry, *Resource and Reference Guide* (True Colors, Inc., 1990).

Don Lowry, *Keys to Personal Success* (True Colors, Inc., 1988).

Don Lowry, *Character Cards* (True Colors, Inc., Communication Companies International, 1988).

Don Lowry, *Parent Cards* (True Colors, Inc., Communication Companies International, 1990).

About True Colors

Our vision at True Colors is to foster positive, healthy, productive communities whose successes flow from the natural dedication of each person. Our powerful, customized "edutainment" workshops, books, workbooks, videos, live shows and events have empowered millions of people during the past twenty years and helped to realize this vision.

Listed below are some of the True Colors resources people across the country are turning to for improved communication in their personal and professional lives.

Also available from True Colors:

True Success in a Career
ISBN 1-893320-24-3

Written specifically for today's teens, **True Success in a Career** introduces high school students to the True Colors process and guides them toward careers that fit with who they are. Author Carolyn Kalil leads students through a journey of self-discovery to help them gain a better understanding of their natural strengths and identify careers in which they will find true satisfaction. 110 pages.

TCB-030 .... $22.95*

Showing Our True Colors
ISBN 1-893320-23-5

Filled with easy-to-use tools for personal growth, this delightfully illustrated book by communication expert Mary Miscisin uncovers the power of the True Colors process. You will discover the characteristics behind each of the four True Colors, as well as tips for understanding, appreciating, and relating to each Color style. Its simple format, charming anecdotes, and convenient reference lists make **Showing Our True Colors** a fun and easy read. And the end result will be a celebration of the uniqueness in yourself and others. 242 pages.

TCB-020 .... $19.95*

More creative resources from True Colors . . .

Dare to Dream

ISBN 1-893320-21-9

Super Bowl champ Curt Marsh challenges readers to dig deep and pursue their dreams, whatever their circumstances. Curt talks about the physical and emotional pain he endured when a football injury led to the amputation of his right foot and ankle. And he shares many of the life lessons that have inspired him to rise above his challenges and pursue his passions—including the True Colors process. **Dare to Dream** will inspire you to embrace change and diversity, discover true toughness, set goals and develop plans to achieve them, and much more! 122 pages.

TCB-010 . . . . **$19.95***

Meaningful Conversations-Connecting the DOT and True Colors.

ISBN 1-893320-26-x

This inspirational book helps educators rediscover the magic of reaching the hearts of students. Educator and author Ann Kashiwa reveals how to identify the True Colors of students and use that information to connect with the core of each child for maximized success in the classroom. A must read for educators of all backgrounds and grade levels. And parents, too!

TCB-050 . . . . **$19.95***

The Sports Management Journal

ISBN 1-885221-97-5

The Sports Management Journal is an easy-to-use workbook written specifically for school coaches and parents of children in sports. Author Cliff Gillies presents tear-out exercises to copy and use in daily coaching and parenting. You'll also find a proven design for coach-parent teaming, games for teaching respectful communication, charts for athletic achievement and improvement, the True Colors personality assessment system and cards, and much more! 179 pages.

TCB-061 . . . . **$14.95***

Action & Communication Guide - for Teachers and Parents

Our popular **Action & Communication Guide** will help identify the "personality" of your classroom and provide effective ways to help you better relate to each student. Features four "colorized" sections—one for each personality type in an easy to use sprial bound book. 88 pages chock full of valuable insight for creating a stimulating classroom environment, motivating learning and achievement, gaining cooperation and more!

TCP230 .... $34.95*

*** Plus shipping and handling**

To order additional copies of

True Parenting or

any of these True Colors products,

please contact us at:

True Colors, Inc.
3605 W. MacArthur Blvd. # 702,
Santa Ana, California 92704

Telephone: (800) 422-4686 or (714) 437-5426
Facsimile (866) 374-8958

E-Mail: info@true-colors.com

Web Site: www.true-colors.com